TURN YOUR PASSION INTO YOUR PROFESSION

To Crystal,

I pray God opens doors for your gifts to manifest.

Your gifts will bring you before great men.

Hope you enjoy reading this.

🙂 . 🙂

06/01/13

To order more copies of this book, please visit www.opyonas.com

TURN YOUR PASSION INTO YOUR PROFESSION

The Step by Step process of turning a simple idea into a Business Venture

OPY ONAS

Turn Your Passion Into Your Profession
Copyright© 2012 Opy Onas.
All rights reserved.

First paperback edition printed in 2012 in the United Kingdom
A catalogue record for this book is available from the British Library.

ISBN 978-0-9574382-0-0

Published by Proten Publishing House

For more copies of this book, please email: info@protenuk.com
Tel: 02071837328

Cover designed by Rhics Studios (www.rhicsstudios.com)

Book Formatted by Nick Asamoah (www.nickasamoah.com)

Printed and bound in the UK by Lightning Source UK Ltd.

This book is dedicated to my beautiful wife, Bose Onaboye and my daughter, Hannah Onaboye who is currently in the womb as I am finishing off this book. Bose, thank you for being a great supporter and cheerleader throughout the good and rough times we've been through. You are my inspiration and the reason I do what I do.

I love you and Hannah.

Table of contents

Acknowledgements   ix

Foreword   xiii

Preface   xv

Why Do New Businesses Fail   1

Step 1 – Find your winning Business idea   9

Step 2 – Create Your Business Identity   19

Step 3 – Check the Viability of Your idea   53

Step 4 – Create Your Long / Short Term goals   75

Step 5 – Differentiate Your Products / Services   85

Step 6 – Choose Your Business Location   91

Step 7 – Define Your Customers   99

Step 8 – Find Your Customers   113

Step 9 – Choose Your Business Premises   125

Step 10 – Explore Your Competitors   137

Step 11 – Explore Your SWOT   145

Step 12 – Set Your Prices   159

Step 13 – Create Your Elevator Pitch   167

Step 14 – Find Your Source of Finance   179

Step 15 – Know Your Numbers   193

Get Up and Do Something   225

Afterword   229

Acknowledgements

It has taken just over a year to get this book from the point of conception, as an idea that came about while jogging on a Saturday morning, to this stage where it has become a finished written book. It has not been easy as I have had to write and edit over and over again, testing a lot of the concepts mentioned in the book through the Business Academy that I set up and various means. To say that the process of getting this book out has been all my own effort would be untrue. There have been some amazing people who have come along to guide, support, push and motivate as well as encourage me through the tough times when I felt like giving up.

The top of the list of acknowledgements would be God. Everything I have and all that I possess has been given to me by God from above, my gift of inspiration and motivation, as well as my writing skills are all gifts from God in order to help others. I thank the Lord for seeing me through the ups and downs of putting together this book.My next acknowledgement would be my extended family. Apart from my wife who has been a rock for me throughout my Entrepreneurial journey, I have been blessed with an amazing family on both my side and my wife's. I have four amazing sisters who I love dearly. I would like to thank my oldest sister Esther Adenusi. Apart from my wife, she has been my biggest cheerleader. Even though she didn't fully understand the concept of 'Coaching' nor had a great understanding of what I do, she always believed that I would be successful at whatever I do. For that reason, I would like to say thank you for the days when she would encourage me to keep going. I cannot thank Esther without mentioning her husband, James Adenusi; thank you for your support. I would also like to acknowledge my three other sisters, Fay, Sherry and Elizabeth. I love you all and thank you for being great sisters to me in times of need.

I cannot be the man I am today without my Dad, James Onaboye. I learnt so much from him while growing up. He taught me to stand for what I believe, work hard, look after my family and put God first in all I do. This is the reason why I have been able to get to this point in life. The joy on my Dad's face whenever he sees my article in a newspaper is priceless. I would also like to acknowledge my mum, who I love dearly; I also dedicate this book to her as she has been through so much in life and yet never stopped being a caring mum to me. I cannot mention my extended family without acknowledging my mother-in-law, Victoria Asade. Since I've been married to Bose, she has always treated me like a son. She believed in me enough to allow me to marry her daughter even when I had nothing. Thank you. Finally I would like to acknowledge my brother-in-law Jibola Gbago. He is also one of the people that have encouraged me along the Entrepreneurial journey. To find a brother-in-law who would support you when times are tough is not easy. Not forgetting his wife Dami Gbago, thank you for your continual support.

I have always maintained and shared openly that I wouldn't be anywhere near where I am today if I didn't have great mentors who have helped and supported me along the way. I would like to acknowledge one of my closest friends, brother and mentor, Samson Baptiste. Samson is probably one of the few people that could tell the full details of the journey towards completing this book. He always has time to listen my moaning, give me good advice and encourage me. Thank you for all you've done for me Samson, I really appreciate it. Secondly I would like to acknowledge a couple who have known me from the very start of my entrepreneurial journey and they are also like a brother and sister to me. Joyce and Agyeman Duah, thank you for your continual support and encouragement towards me and my family as a whole. Gbenga Ajewole, thank you for also supporting my journey. You were one of the first few people to see the first couple of pages of this book and you immediately told me that it was very good. Thank You!

When it comes to Business, there was a man who saw me once and decided to invest his own money in me because he saw potential in me. He invested hundreds of pounds in me after meeting me for the first time and till date he has continued to be an inspiration, mentor and brother to me. Raymond McMillan, you are a star! I really cannot tell you how much I value you both as a friend and mentor. I would also like to thank other mentors that have come into my life at one stage or the other. These are people who have taught me certain concepts which I have applied in this book. A huge thanks to Alnur Dhanani who agreed to mentor and offer me his time; guiding and supporting me in the right path, Paul Simister who taught me a lot about coaching when I started off and Brad Burton who gave me a big push at the conception of the idea for the Business Start-Up Academy. Other mentors also include Johnny Apples and the list goes on. Thank you.

As a Business owner, there is nothing more important than having people who you can bounce your ideas off. Thank you to Roger Black who has also been a mentor to me, offering his time to sit down with me and hear my 'crazy' ideas for taking over the world. How I met Roger was quite funny but that can't be told in this book. Finally, I would like to acknowledge a dear friend and mentor, Ade Shokoya. Ade met with me and sparked the passion to pick up my laptop and finish off this book. Thank you for pushing me towards my dreams and always giving time to support me right from the start.

As I have mentioned earlier, a lot of content in this book had to be tried and tested before I released them in order to ensure that they worked. One of the ways of doing this was trying out the content at the Business Start-Up Academy. There are certain people who heavily supported me through the launch and delivery of the first ever Business-start-up Academy. I would like to thank and acknowledge Pastor Des and Sue Figueiredo. They supported the launch of the Academy as well as the running of the first course at the Academy. Thank You! Thank you for also supporting me and Bose throughout our time at the church and availing yourself to support us. I would also like to thank the whole Balham Community Church congregation. When I was organising the launch event for the Academy, the whole church joined hands to help market, spread the word, serve and ensure that the event was a success and I thank you all.

I also acknowledge the Resurrection Power Church leaders under whom I grew up through my teenage years and early twenties. Thank you to Pastor Price David, Aaron Armah, Chris Yeboah and the other leaders for the help and support. I am where I am today because of your support and contribution in different ways.

I always believe that it is essential to surround yourself with the right people when going through your entrepreneurial journey. I couldn't have continued pursuing my dreams without great friends. I want to acknowledge friends such as Prar Eshun, a great friend and brother who has heavily supported me from the first day I ever had a Business idea. He created my logos, marketing materials, photo shoot and many other things. Chris Nwaigwe, my trusted web and graphic designer. He never lets me down and he has always helped me at the tough times. Sandra and Nicholas Asamoah, my great media team, thank you. You both rock. Apart from being great friends, you have been great supporters. Thank You! Opeyemi Ilesanmi, a great childhood friend who always supports me in everything that I do. Thanks for standing by me and being a great friend when others didn't.
There are also many great friends who have heavily supported my dream from the start such as Muriel Obeng, Elsie Senam, Shirley De Lawrence, Nina Bobie Agyekum, Karen Adoo, Toyosi Ogedengbe, Emmanuel Dare Anthony and many others who have supported in one way or the other.

I would like to acknowledge certain companies that have helped with the bringing together of this book, whether through editing the content or help with creating the design etc. Alfred A Malnick Accountancy Services, thank you for editing the section on finances. Rhics Web Studios, thank you for helping with the websites. Prareshun.com, thanks for the photo shoot. PicsVid ltd, thanks for always supplying my multimedia equipments at every event and seminar I have hosted. The team at BNI Academy thanks for the continual support throughout my journey.
My company cannot grow or become successful without great clients. Thank you to all the clients that we have worked with over the years. It has been a privilege to work with you. Thank you to the first clients that I coached, for believing in me

enough to pay for my time. Thank you to everyone who has been to our Academy and those who continually refer me on to friends.

Finally, I would like to thank others who I may not have mentioned but have always inspired me, believed in me or encouraged me in one way or the other to never give up. Thank you!

To those who thought I was crazy for pursuing my passion and I would never make it or get anywhere, I would like to acknowledge you too and say thanks for motivating me and indirectly pushing me forward.

Foreword

Having met Opy Onas a couple of years ago, I was impressed by his determination and drive to create a real change and help individuals achieve their potentials. It's been very inspiring to see the transition he has made in his life and how he has turned his own passion into his profession. I have had the opportunity of mentoring him over the last few years and supported him towards the completion of this book. 'Turn Your Passion into Your Profession' is a book that has been written for the modern day aspiring entrepreneur. Having started a few businesses myself, I've experienced the many challenges entrepreneurs have to face during the start-up phases and having a book like this will make this process very easy.

Written for individuals with little or no previous Business experience at all, one of the first things immediately noticeable about this book is the simplicity of the concepts covered in each chapter - and even with my many years of being in business it is always great to be reminded of the basic fundamentals of starting a new Business.

The release of this book is timely right now because more people are 'taking the plunge' and opting for self-employment, making this book a valuable asset to anyone who is serious about doing something about their Business idea.
So read it, digest it – and act upon it.

Ade Shokoya
Founder, AgileTV.com
Author, Waterfall to Agile: A Practical Guide to Agile Transition

<u>Preface</u>

The critical ingredient is getting off your butt and doing something. It's as simple as that. A lot of people have ideas, but there are few who decide to do something about them now. Not tomorrow. Not next week. But today. The true entrepreneur is a doer, not a dreamer.

NOLAN BUSHNELL

As I put the finishing touches to this book, ready to be published, I look back at the last year and a smile comes to my face. I remember how I started putting together this book and how it was once an idea I had in my mind. It all started one Saturday in August when I went jogging early in the morning. I had a 'light bulb moment'. I wanted to write up a workbook which would be used to run workshops and programmes, making it easy for individuals to go from an idea to a venture.
As a Business coach, I am constantly approached by individuals with the same problem and question:

"I have an idea but I don't know that to do about it"
Many individuals have approached me, asking me about the next step to take with their ideas and I thought to myself,'Wouldn't it be great to have a book that will solve this problem?'

I wanted to write a book which can be used by even the most 'un-business minded' individual to take a simple idea to the next level. This is exactly what this book is about. It has been designed to give you simple steps, coupled with action tasks, which will help you apply the concepts discussed to your own idea.
In the last couple of years, the economic climate in the financial world has been tough and this has led to a lot of job losses and redundancies. Many people who have depended on the comfort and security of being in a regular job are finding themselves scratching their heads and looking for the next move.

For some, this has given them an opportunity to explore their hidden talents, discover inner gifts or pick up their scrap books and look at the viability of the idea which they have tucked away for a long time due to lack of motivation for pursuing it and turning it into a successful venture. It has been said that most Businesses are birthed during a recession and this has become very evident from the emergence of numerous amount of new Businesses starting up.

'Turn Your Passion into Your Profession' is not a textbook, story book or even an average Business book. It is designed to be a practical guide for anyone with a Business idea. It doesn't matter what stage you are with your idea, you can still apply the principles in this book to your Business. The principles discussed in this book can be applied whether you are a group or an individual:

- Who has the desire to become a Business owner but doesn't know how or where to start from.

- Who has an idea and wants to 'know how' to turn the idea into a Business venture.

- Who has just started a new Business and wants to develop a good foundation for your Business.

- Who is an existing Business owner who wants to revisit the basic principles of your Business.

This book should not be read like a novel, nor should it be rushed when reading it: It has been designed to be worked through, chapter by chapter. The best way to use this book is to go through each chapter, read the contents, understand it and think about how you can apply them to your own idea. The questions in the action tasks have been structured in a way to draw out information which you may not usually think about and it helps you to structure your idea in a way that will allow you to use it in pursuing your Business venture.

This book is not a Business plan and it has not been designed to imitate a Business plan. It has been designed to help you in creating your Business plan and all the information covered in this book will enable you to fully understand your idea and convert the information derived through this book to either make up your Business plan or actualize it when starting your Business.

This book has been compiled using several research sources and consulting with several experts who have been acknowledged in different sections. It is important to note that the action tasks that accompany each chapter will allow you to apply the principles discussed in this book to your own Business idea.

Everyone, to some extent, has a Business idea which they would like to pursue at some point in their life. Some people end up pursuing their ideas, turning them into successful ventures while others live their lives without taking the opportunity and pursuing the ideas. This book has been designed to allow you not only to turn that idea into a Business venture, but also to look at the viability of your idea. It will allows you to answer three key questions:

- Is my idea going to work?

- What do I need to 'tweak' to make this idea work?

- What is the long term sustainability of my idea?

As much as it is good to receive general Business advice and guidance, you must note that every Business is unique and you may not be able to get a tailored guide that can be applied to your specific Business idea. This is why this self coaching guide has been supplied with accompanied tasks that not only allows you to read and understand the principles discussed in this book but also allows you to examine ways which it can be applied to your unique idea.

I hope this book truly makes a difference to your life and it helps you get out of your comfort zone and bring that conceived idea into reality.

WHY DO NEW BUSINESSES FAIL?

"By failing to prepare, you are preparing to fail"

BENJAMIN FRANKLIN

Before diving into the subject of starting a new Business, it is important to look at some of the reasons why a new Business can fail. **Facts gathered over the years have shown that 50 percent of new Businesses fail within the first year while a further 90-95 percent fail within the first five years.**

From my experience of working with different types of individuals as well as having the privilege of coming across several great ideas, it is always sad to see a Business start up which never makes it past the first 6 month to 1 year. There are many reasons for this and we will examine those in this chapter.

As a new Business owner or a prospective start-up, it is important for you to be aware of the common mistakes made by these failed Businesses as it can ensure that you do not fall into the same category. Starting a new Business can be compared with driving a car. It cannot be fully learnt and understood theoretically, it has to be practised. You cannot avoid every mistake in Business, but it is always good to learn from others in order to minimise the mistakes and 'bumps' which you may experience along the way. You may have a few 'scratches and dents' while starting off, but you have to learn to enjoy the experience and learn from every mistake.

Back to the reasons why new Businesses fail; after conducting a research with a number of people and looking at some examples of Businesses that have failed to take off, here are some of the top reasons why new Businesses fail:

• Incompetent Owner: It is said that Businesses don't fail, the owners do. Majority of Businesses that fail may have succeeded if they were run by the right people. There are several examples of Businesses that have nearly gone into the drain and all it took was a change in the CEO or ownership and the company was revived.

Example

Apple Inc was facing the prospect of Bankruptcy after Steve Jobs left the company in 1985. When he was brought back into the company in 1997, he was able to revive the company and Apple has become a global name, dominating both the Smartphone, tablet and computer hardware industry.

As a Business owner, it is important to develop the right mindset and ensure that you are leading the company in the right direction. A Business owner who is incompetent will only lead the company to ruins. It's advisable to find a coach, mentor or Business advisor who will ensure that you are running your Business effectively.

• **Lack of Long Term Vision**: One of the most common reasons for new Business failure is that Business owners do not have a long term vision for the company. A vision is different from a plan. A plan allows you to achieve a goal or vision. Plans will always change as you start running your Business, but your goal or vision will always stay the same as it guides you to ensure that all the steps you are taking are in line with your Business. Failing to establish a clear vision will only lead you in several directions. When you understand where you are taking your company in 5-10 years or even within the first year, this will enable you to persevere through difficult periods in the first year where many people tend to give up.

Having a long term vision will also allow you to effectively integrate new staff members, partners and any other new members into the Business as you will be able to share the goal and vision of the company with them. We will look at the issue of creating a clear vision later on in this book and you will learn the importance of having a clearly defined vision.

• **Insufficient planning**: This is one of the areas where you are likely to get people with different points of view. There are people who believe in meticulously planning before stepping out to run their Business, while there are others who believe in 'just getting on with it'.

In my experience with start-ups, I have met people who have taken two years to write a Business Plan and keep it tucked away nicely on a shelf without actualizing the plans. I believe that it is important to have a sufficient plan / strategy and take the first step. As I mentioned earlier, it is impossible to avoid every single mistake in running a Business but you can minimize the challenges that you will face by taking time out to research your market and the product or service which you will be delivering.

The key to success is not developing a great Business plan but having the ability to adapt to changes that may occur which may cause deviation from your Business plan.

There are many examples of great Business owners who started off their Businesses without a formal Business plan, but eventually as the company began to grow, started developing a plan of action in order to have a smooth transition. Business plans are essential in certain situations, such as applying for bank loans or acquiring investments from private investors.

Sufficient planning will enable you to understand how to go from point A to point B. It will allow you to state your strategy for achieving your sales figures as well as understanding the projected turnover for your company.

• **Wrong Location:** Placing your Business in the wrong location can cause it to fail even from the beginning. It is important to know that your location is an important factor to consider because you must make sure that you are situated in an area where either your target market are located, or an area which is easy to be accessed by your customers, employees and suppliers. If you place your Business premises in an area that is inaccessible, it maybe difficult to make sufficient sales. The choice of your Business location must be taken even more seriously if your Business requires a lot of face to face interaction. A whole section of this book has been dedicated to helping you choose your Business location.

• **Lack of capital:** There is a simple saying which goes:

"When there is no money, the dream dies"

One of the most common mistakes which aspiring entrepreneurs make is the inability to find sufficient capital needed to fund their Business start-up. It is true that you can start a Business with little or no capital, but your Business will need some injection of capital at a certain stage. You must understand the amount of capital needed to start off your Business. Lack of capital will certainly destroy a Business as it means that the Business owner is unable to acquire the required resources to operate in the Company. Your first step is to define your start-up cost and start looking at your source of funding. This book will show you how to do these in the upcoming chapters.

• **No clear target market:** Failing to identify your main target market is like shooting a gun in the sky and hoping that a bird would fly by so you can hit it. If you fail to fully understand your target market, you are likely to attract no one and lack of customers will only lead to lack of sales. One of the first steps which we take with new clients in our company is to ensure that we fully understand their target market. As a Business owner, failure to identify your target audience means that you are unable to create a targeted marketing campaign, you cannot develop a strategy and it will be difficult to create a brand which will attract the right people to your products or services.

• **Lack of required skills and knowledge:** This is one of the factors which pertain to you as the Business owner. It is important for you to go into a Business where you have adequate knowledge about the industry. You may start a Business where you will employ the skills of others to carry out the job, but it is essential that you still have enough knowledge about that particular industry as the owner of the Business.

Example

You may decide to start up a cleaning company. You do not have to know how to clean in order to start up the Business, but you must have enough knowledge about the cleaning industry, understand the machinery that is needed, the process involved in securing contracts etc.

You must ensure that your skills and knowledge are up to date. There is so much free information and ways to build new skills that there is no excuse for not acquiring the skills needed.

• **Advertising**: Advertising is essential to any Business. It is important that you constantly create exposure about your products or services to your potential customers or target market. If you start a Business and you fail to consistently advertise yourself, you will lose your potential customers to your competitor down the road.

Advertising does not merely consist of dropping a flier through your customer's door once a year, but it has to be repeated constantly. Many of your customers will not buy your products until they have seen your marketing material over and over again.

• **Lack of Support or Network**: Starting a new Business can be lonely, especially if you are starting off as a 'one man band'. Sitting in your home office or working from your office space by yourself can get frustrating and lonely. Therefore it is important to build a network of other Business owners around you.

As a start-up, it is important that you attend regular networking events in order to ensure that you are surrounding yourself with people who can support you and also build networks that can help grow your Business. Your first big business deal could just be waiting for you at the next networking event in your area.
This is also one of the advantages of having a coach as a start-up; it ensures that you have the right support through the process. Starting a new Business can be a very tough process, especially in the first couple of years when you may not get the positive result expected but keeping yourself in the right network will certainly ease the pressure.

Trying to do it all by yourself will only frustrate you and can lead to succumbing to the pressure and eventually giving up.

• **Lack of time/attention:** One of the most difficult situations is where an individual is trying to juggle a start up while in full time job. Starting up a new Business requires time and dedication. You may find it tough to start your new Business while still in a full time employment, it is therefore important to set apart at least 1 hour a day to working on your Business.

At the start-up phase, you have to ensure that the right foundations are laid, you are building your contacts and you are meeting your sales target. These activities take time and this is one of the reasons why it is important to be accountable to a coach or mentor.

If you find yourself struggling with your time management due to different issues, it is important that you address these issues as poor time management can destroy your Business.

• **Not enough demand:** Customers are the lifeblood of any Business. This factor ties in to the choice of Business location. If you chose to locate your Business in an area saturated with your competitors, you must ensure that there is enough demand in that area.

Setting up your Business in an area where there is not enough demand for the competition in the area will only lead to fewer sales and eventually close down your Business.

One of the Businesses which do not tend to face this challenge are fast food restaurants, convenience stores and other Businesses that supply essential products which will always be in high demand.

• **Lack of of Perseverance:** My definition of perseverance is the ability to consistently keep the right standard and do the right thing in any given situation despite challenges, oppositions or how you feel.

As mentioned earlier, many Businesses could have survived if they were owned by different individuals. One of the main reasons why Businesses do not make it past the start up stage is that the owners give up too quickly before they see the fruits of their hard work.

This is also linked to lack of vision and plan. Having a vision means that you are able to project how long it will take you to reach your destination and this will also allow you to be patient along the way. There is no denying the fact that running a Business is not a 'stroll in the park', however, once you have built a solid foundation for your Business, it is easier to build upon it.

The points mentioned are only the most popular ones and you may think of other factors which haven't been mentioned but the main focus is to be aware and understand the factors which may contribute to the downfall of your new Business.

We will dive deeper into some of these factors and examine how you can tackle them for your new Business.

ACTION POINTS

After reading some of my reasons why new Businesses fail. I would like you to pick up a pen and your notebook and write down other reasons which haven't been mentioned in this chapter which can also contribute to the failure of a new Business.

STEP 1

FIND YOUR WINNING IDEA

"Business opportunities are like buses, there's always another one coming"

RICHARD BRANSON

After looking at some of the reasons why many new Businesses fail, we can now go ahead and examine the first step to turning your passion into your Profession. When thinking about becoming a Business owner, the first step is to find an idea. Opportunities are all around you, the most important thing is to recognise these opportunities and grab them.

At this point, it can be assumed that you have decided to become a Business owner and you either have an idea already or you are looking for ideas which you can turn into a Business venture. Whatever stage you are in, it is still important to understand some of the ways to find a winning Business idea. You may find that you will continue to modify your Business idea along your entrepreneurial journey and you may even change the original idea, therefore it is important to be aware of the ways of coming up with different ideas.

If you are a new Business owner or an individual who has already chosen an idea, then this chapter will help you establish and re-evaluate the idea. The beauty of Business ideas is that they tend to change over time or they are likely to adapt to changes in the environment, therefore as a Business owner or aspiring Entrepreneur, you must ensure that you are able to adapt to any change that occurs to your idea and you are always willing to modify your idea at any time in order to adapt to any changes in the environment. When I talk about changes in the environment, I'm referring to legal, economical, social, political or technological changes that may occur which would have an impact on your Business.

As previously mentioned, as an entrepreneur you must be able to spot a good Business idea from afar.

Example

You must be able to spot opportunities where everyone else sees a problem. For example, if you regularly use a dry-cleaners and you find it quite annoying to keep going up and down to pick up your clothes from the dry cleaners, you could either see this as an annoying problem or this could give you an opportunity to open up a dry cleaners which will pick up and deliver the clothes to be cleaned and hence solving your problem.

One of the most important points about any Business idea is that it it must be solving one problem or the other and people must be willing to pay for it. These are some of the fundamental factors that determine the viability of an idea.

When looking at the idea of starting a new Business from scratch, it can sometimes be a daunting experience for you if you have not previously owned a Business of your own and it is important to fully understand what you are trying to achieve in your Business venture as a new owner. We are going to discuss this is more detail when looking at your Business identity but we are first going to examine ways by which you can find that winning idea for your new Business. In order to create a new Business from scratch, it starts with an idea which comes from a problem which you have spotted and there are several ways to spot Business ideas.

A quick and easy way to find your Business idea is to ask yourself this question: *"If I was given £5000 and I was told to use it to set up either a new Business, a project or any type of venture that will generate more money, what would I do."* The money cannot be put in a bank, nor can it be used to buy stocks or shares, it has to be used to develop a new venture

Here are some of the methods that you can use to find your new Business idea:

<u>From a Passion or Hobby</u>

One of the first things you should do when thinking of an idea is to look at what you love doing, what you are good at and what you can't go one day without thinking about. For some people, it might be just to organise stuff, some people find it easy to counsel and listen to others, some love writing while others love painting. Whatever your hobby is, you must recognise it and find out how this can be packaged into a product or service which can be offered to the public and add value to others.

When we talk about your passion or hobbies, we are referring to those things which you naturally find yourself doing, something which you are good at, something which you constantly think about and you do effortlessly. You may find it hard to recognise your passion, this is not uncommon; many people find it difficult to pinpoint what they are particularly passionate about. Here are some of the ways to identify your passion:

1. Indentify the things that get you excited: Ask yourself these questions:

    i. What gets me excited?
    ii. What do I get a kick out of doing?
    iii. What do I have fun doing?
    iv. What do I always love doing even if I don't get paid for it?

When you ask yourself these questions, it could be something as simple as networking with people or meeting new people. Don't discount your hobby or passion. List down all the things which gets you excited at the thought of doing it. Here is an analogy that can help you; if you were in a room where people were having different conversations and you overheard a conversation on a particular topic which grabs your attention and you immediately want to get involved in that topic. What would this topic be? This will give you a clue to the things which gets you excited.

2. Look back at your childhood: This is another way to find out what your passion is. When growing up, there would have been certain traits which you would have found out about yourself or something others continually told you about. For example, your family members may have been telling you that you have a passion for inspiring people to success and you would still have the same passion which you can then look to turn into a Business venture.

3. List down your talents: Your talents are those things which come naturally to you, those things which you do not have to struggle to achieve. The same things may be hard for others to do, but those things will always come easy for you. What you may need to do is take a piece of paper and list down all your talents. You can either do this by listing down your talents yourself or asking people who are close to you, what they think your talents are.

4. Explore your current job: If you're currently working in a corporate environment. This is an opportunity to test out your skills and look at where your skills fit in best in the different departments. In your workplace, you can ask to try out different departments to see where you fit in best and this will help to examine what your true passion is as an individual. This will help you to look at where your passion can be used in a Business environment.

5. What do you constantly read about: Everybody takes information in one way or the other. Some people enjoy reading books, some enjoy magazines or newspapers while others enjoy reading articles online. What you also need to think about when trying to explore your passion is to look at the content of the information which you constantly read. This will allow you to know what your interests are.

6. Look at your education or Qualification: Another way of finding out your passion is to look back at your education orthe qualifications which you have attained. You may find that there are particular subject areas which you enjoyed studying and through your education, you have developed an interest in these subject area. For example, you may not have thought about computer programming until your studied it in university and found out that you actually enjoyed it as a subject and you can therefore use this knowledge and interest to develop a Business venture that involved developing different types of computer software for companies.

One of the biggest mistakes you can make is to take your talent or gift for granted. Many people assume that just because they find it easy to do something means that other people find it easy to do the same thing or nobody will place any value on it.

When you either go into a workplace or look at a comparison of several Business owners, you can tell those who are passionate about their Business or career and those who do it for the sake of money or other reasons. It is said that:

'When you do something that you love, you will never work another day.'

When you are driven by your passion, you will wake up every day always looking forward to serving your customers. When you look at successful entrepreneurs, one of the traits which you will see is the fact that they are passionate about what they do and they are constantly looking at better ways to serve their customers.

<u>ACTION POINTS</u>

After finding out the different ways of recognising your passion, the next step is to apply these concepts to yourself. Take your notebook and pen and list down all your passion using the points which have been given to you. If you are struggling to recognise your passion, ask others who may know you very well and show them the pointers which have been given above.

<u>Spot a gap in the market</u>

The second thing that can be adopted in your quest for a winning idea is to spot a gap in an existing market. A market refers to the total amount of potential or actual buyers of your products or service. Therefore when we talk about spotting a gap in the market, this refers to identifying a particular segment or demography that may need your products or service but do not currently have access to it.

Example
You may be a fan of Caribbean food and you realise that your new area does not currently have any Caribbean restaurants. This immediately springs up as an opportunity for you to serve the market in that area which is not being catered for as long as you are sure that there is a demand.

A gap could also exist in the form of a target market. For example, you could decide to sell fashion clothing especially targeted at the older market aged 70 and over. You could have looked into the fashion industry and realise that this market is lacking a very good representation so your brand could be targeted at them. The main point is to look at the market which you are about to enter and think about a gap that is not being catered for or a gap which has not been populated by competition. Spotting a gap requires you to be very vigilant and alert to the segments of your market that may be ignored by existing products and you will then tap into this space.

Look at the industry which you are interested in or look at general products which are already out there and examine their target market. Ask yourself these questions:

- What products can I take and tailor to a different type of market?
- What products currently exist out there that do not serve every single type of audience but has a demand from all kinds of buyers?

An example of bringing an existing product into a new market can be seen with the introduction of shaving sticks specifically for women. Shaving sticks existed before this but they were generally targeted at men. Pink shaving sticks were then invented which targeted the female market and the design and features of the shaving stick were designed to appeal to the female market.

ACTION POINTS

List down examples of products or services which currently exists but can be taken and tailored to a different type of market. Remember that products can be tailored to a different market segment if they can be brought into a different location.

Spot a missing feature in an existing product or service

This is one of the most common ways which inventors use in developing a new concept. Sometimes an existing product is missing a feature that could make it better or add value to its user and you have to be able to spot this missing feature.

Example

Imagine that you need to have your suit and shirt dry-cleaned for work and you realise that the dry cleaners are closed by the time you arrive back from work. This poses a problem for you as it means that you are unable to drop your items at the dry cleaners to be washed.

The solution may be to start-up a dry cleaners which offers home delivery and pick up service which makes it convenient for busy individuals to get their clothes cleaned.

The example above demonstrates how you can spot a missing feature in an existing product. This method goes back to the point that was previously made about being able to spot an opportunity. The next time you buy a product or you experience a service and you complain about it, it may be an opportunity for you to offer the same service with an improvement by adding the features which are missing.

How many times have you bought a product and complained about its functionality, lifespan, quality or presentation? When you buy a product or you are offered a service, always look for a missing feature or element to it. With the rise of technology, products are constantly evolving and new features are being added to products and services which are supplied by several companies e.g. the mobile phones that were first invented were made with no access to the internet but as time went on, mobile phone companies decided to add features such as instant internet and now we have seen the rapid expansion of the PDA phones.

This is another example of looking at existing products or services and looking for missing elements which can be added to them. Decide that whenever people are complaining about a product or idea, you will find ways to create an opportunity out of this.

ACTION POINTS

Look at the recent items which you have purchased or services which you have experienced and list down the features that may be added to these items in order to improve them in different ways.

Spot a market which is rapidly growing in demand

The fourth method that can be utilised in finding your next Business idea is to spot a market that is rapidly increasing. As mentioned earlier, a market refers to the potential or actual buyers of a product or service. Therefore when referring to an expanding market, this refers to a product or service whose demand is increasing.

Example

A market which is growing in demand is the Tablet computer market that was once dominated by Apple Computers. Once other manufacturers realised that the market is growing, they also developed tablets and tapped into the market that was emerging with increasing demand and this is evident now with different suppliers developing their own brands of tablet PCs.

This is another reason why people go into Business. Another example is the hair extensions market in the UK. This is a market which is expanding as more females are spending more money on hair extensions and the industry is thought to be worth around 9 billion pounds. With this astonishing figure which keeps increasing, it is obvious that the market has a lot of demand for its products. Therefore you may decide to set up a Business which engages in this type of product, but in order to do so, you must have the necessary knowledge and passion needed to enter the industry and you must also have a degree of passion for the type of product.

It is highly risky to step into a market just because it has a lot of demand as you can end up losing interest in the business if the demands die down. Hence it is important to have some passion for the Business which you are getting involved in. Your business must be giving you more fulfilment that a financial reward.

It is however important to keep an eye out for increasing demand in an industry or market which you may be interested in as demand for products or services will depend on several external factors such as economic climate, Government policies etc. A perfect example of this is the housing market which seems to fluctuate in demand based on the economic climate.

ACTION POINTS

Write down at least ten types of markets that you have noticed with an increase in demand. If possible, look at the industry which you have an interest in.

These are just some of the methods which you can use when looking for that new idea that you can turn into a Business venture. There are other ways of acquiring a new Business such as:

• Buying a Business Franchise
• Buying an Existing Business
• Multilevel / Network Marketing

The main focus of this book is to guide you through the process of developing your own ideas, hence why it is not treating the other methods.

ACTION POINTS

Write down other ways of finding a new Business idea. You may have some other methods which have not been mentioned. Write them down and examine them in order to create your winning idea.

STEP 2

CREATE YOUR BUSINESS IDENTITY

"An image is not simply a trademark, a design, a slogan or an easily remembered picture. It is a studiously crafted personality profile of an individual, institution, corporation, product or service"

DANIEL J BOORSTIN

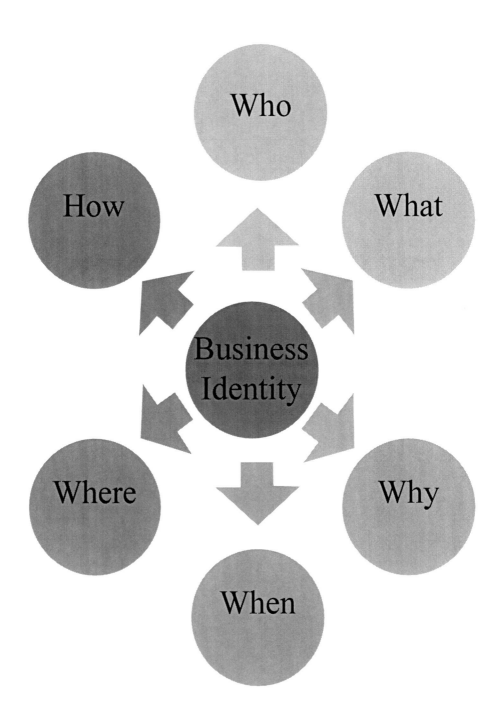

When thinking about turning your passion into your profession, there are certain things that you must first consider. Many people rush into starting a Business without laying the right foundations for the Business. Just like a house needs a good foundation, so does a good Business.

Every individual is born with an identity and every object has attributes by which you can identify it. Your identity is what makes you unique as an individual and sets you apart from everyone else. Without an identity, it is impossible to stand out or be recognised by those who may know you or even start to think about where you fit in society. The same principle applies to objects, every single object has to be identified somehow or else people who are looking for it will not be able to find it.

The same analogy can be applied to your new Business; every Business must have an identity. When we refer to a Business identity, we are talking about the attributes that define the Business. Just like you have attributes that define you as a human being and you use these attributes to identify yourself and in doing so, you are able to identify people who are likeminded. A Business has to recognise its attributes and understand its identity before even progressing any further.

It's amazing how many Businesses start off without clearly defining who they are as a Business and what they are really supposed to be offering to their customers. Understanding your identity as a Business helps you to clearly define a unique brand for your new Business as well as identifying your USP (Unique Selling Point). The issue of your USP will be dealt with in subsequent chapters.

To deal with the issue of creating your Business identity, you must first understand the meaning of the word. Your Business identity can be defined as the characteristics that determine the perception which your Business gives out to its customers, competitors and the industry at large. These are the characteristics that can give you an understanding of your idea as well as giving it a structure.

Without starting off with your Business identity, it will be hard for you to build other aspect of your Business. The identity gives you a starting point which you can then build upon. Take yourself as an individual who for example, before startingto look for a career, must first understand the interests which you want to pursue. Similarly, in order to know the right social circle which you can fit into, you must be aware of your interests. These are just some of the importance of having and knowing your identity.

Here are some of the other benefits to understanding and defining your Business identity:

• Defining your Business identity allows you to easily create the brand and image of your company. Back to the analogy of a human identity, the image that an individual projects will give you an idea of what type of person he or she is. A person's image can either tell you their profession, their interests, age, gender etc. The same applies to a Business. The way in which you present your Business will always send out a message to your intended customers or the market as a whole. With the wrong image sent out to the market, you can either lose the right customers or attract the wrong market, or you can attract the right market and gain more share in your market. Before creating a logo, designing a website, putting out advertising or even speaking to your customers, the first step is to understand your identity and Business concept.

• Understanding your Business identity will allow you to know how to position yourself in your industry and create your USP effectively. One of the main factors that can destroy your Business even from the start is the lack of differentiation. A whole chapter has been dedicated to this subject in this book. Once you understand your identity, you are able to differentiate yourself from your competitors.

• Creating a Business identity will allow you to effectively set long term and short term goals for your company. It is impossible to start setting goals for your company without knowing what your purpose is or what problems you are supposed to be solving in the market place. One of the main reasons why most Businesses do not make it past their first five years is simply because they do not have a long term goal. Your identity will allow you to discover your purpose and therefore explore the long term feasibility of your Business.

• When you have intentionally created an identity, you are able to attract the right type of market to your Business. It's very important that your identity is projected to your intended audience. Let's take a real life example, if you're looking for a life partner and you visit a dating website, there is a particular type of person which you will be looking for and this person must have certain characteristics which will attract you. Let's assume that you are a guy who is interested in a girl aged between 24 and 27, works in a corporate environment, has an Asian ethnicity and of a certain height. When you are searching on the dating site, you will be looking for these characteristics in the people whom you come across and you will probably respond once you find someone who fits some of the characteristics listed. This is the same way that running a Business works. Customers already have an idea of the type of products or services they are looking for and their aim would be to look for a company which can best fulfil that need and if you do not project your identity properly, you will end up losing a potential customer.

• Your identity will allow you to easily identify your competitors. If you do not understand your identity, it is impossible to know who your competitors are because you will not be able to identify someone with similar characteristics as you. Therefore it is highly important to understand your Business identity or else you will fail to know when a new competition arrives in the market and you could be facing a threat without being aware of it.

• As a Business owner, it is imperative that you are able to understand your Business identity in order to be able to communicate the same message to your staff or employees. Whether you are planning to start your Business alone, start with a partner, employ some staff members at the start or fully run the whole Business alone, it is important that you should understand the identity of your Business. If you do not understand this, how can you expect someone else to come on board and understand the concept of the Business?

• As a Business owner, you must be able to confidently talk about your Business and pitch your idea at any given point. This is also where the Business identity comes in. Defining the identity of your Business means that you are able to practise this and use it to clearly describe your company as a whole at any given point including an elevator pitch which will be examined in subsequent chapters of this book. Being able to sell yourself is very important as a new Business owner. If you are not able to confidently and passionately project your Business idea to the listener, they will not buy into your idea. When you are just starting off, you will face situations where people would want to know about your new Business, whether in a networking event, a social gathering, around family members or other occasions, you will always find people who want to know about your new venture, if you sound like you are not sure of what your concept is, it is impossible for people to take you seriously and you could lose a possible referral.

Apart from these few point listed, there are several other reasons why knowing and understanding your Business identity is very important.

When talking about your Business identity, there are 6 key concepts that have to be examined in order to create that identity. These are:

1. Who – The overview of your company.
2. What – Products and Services
3. Why – What problems are you solving?
4. Where – The location of your company and the area of coverage.
5. When – Times of operation.
6. How – Method of operation.

The next step to take is to look at each question in more details and examine how they can be used in creating your Business identity.

<u>WHO - Company Overview</u>

The 'Who' refers to the description of your Business as a whole. There is a difference between the 'who' of your Business and the 'what'. Similarly, there is a difference between 'who' you are as an individual and what you do for a living. Who you are as an individual refers to those attributes that encapsulates your character and can be used to identify you even before you mention what you do. Similarly, in a Business sense, there are certain words which will be associated with your Business even before the customer buys from you.

Whether you are conscious of it or not, as an individual, there are certain words which you would like people to associate with you when they see you, meet you, talk to you or just have a first time glance at you. These are the words that exist in your subconscious mind and they drive your daily decision making: when you dress, speak, walk or relate to other people. These words are used to define you. For example, you could describe someone as being talkative, fun, quiet, outgoing etc. These words can be derived at by studying the person. This is what we mean by your 'definition', those words which you want to be associated with as an individual.

The same principle can be applied to your Business in terms of your Business definition. You must first define those words which you want your potential clients to think about when they come in contact with any aspect of your Business, whether they are walking past your shop, come in contact with your website or simply looking at your logo or business name.

There is an analogy known as the "three words test". This basically refers to the three words which you would like your customers to think about you when they hear about your Business, think about your Business or see your products or services. This is a very important concept because doing this test will allow you to see your Business from the perspective of your customers. Sometimes as a

Business owner, you may think that you are doing great and you are sending the right messages out to your intended market, but until you carry out an exercise such as the 'three words test', you may not be able to see things from the outside point of view.

Example of a 'three words test' are:

When you think of Ferrari, the three words that would spring to mind would probably be:

1. Stylish   2. Italian   3. Fast

Likewise, when you think of the computer company 'Apple', the three words that will probably come to mind are:

1. Innovative   2. Stylish   3. Fun

Your own words for the Companies given in the example may be different but the point is that every company has an idea of the words which they want their customers to think about when their company springs to mind and they intentionally embed these words in their branding, company name, logo, products or service presentation etc.

ACTION POINTS

Using some of the examples given above, list the keywords that you would like your company to be associated with. List down as many keywords as you can. They can be more than three words as you will be using these words later on.

You may be wondering why I'memphasising on the three words test. As a new Business, it is important to make a good start and your communication to your potential customers is paramount.

Another important fact about the Business definition is that it aids you in creating your elevator pitch. You will have a better understanding of an Elevator pitch as you go further in this book.

Once you have listed the keywords to be associated with your Business, you can proceed to create your Company overview. The overview will give an overall description of your company without going into too much detail. It can act as an introduction in different circumstances such as your company website, brochures, flyers, etc.

Here are the steps to take to create your Company Overview:

- Your Business profession: when we talk about your Business profession, this is not the same as the products or services which you offer as a company. For example:

"We are an IT services company."

With that statement, you haven't told the listener what type of IT services which you supply, all you have done is mention your profession or industry without going into details about which type of IT services you actually offer. This is usually the first statement that people will make when you ask them about their company; they will let you know the industry and the profession in which their company is involved before going into details about the type of products or services which they sell.

- Keywords which you want the customers to pick up on: The second part of your company definition will be the keywords which you have mentioned earlier. These keywords will be used to form a sentence which describes your company.

Example

You are a new fashion boutique and you listed the following as words which you want your customers to think about when your company comes to their mind:

1. Fashion   2. Tailored,   3. Handmade   4. Quick   5. Expert.

The next step would be to look at these words and think about how you can incorporate them in a sentence which you can use to describe your company. Below is an example of incorporating the keywords in a sentence:

"We are a new fashion boutique that offers handmade clothing and accessories tailored to your specifications. With our high level of expertise and quality of materials used, we are able to offer quick turnarounds on all orders placed with us. "

Joining the two steps together will help create the first part of your Business identity. Using the two composed sentences, you should be able to describe your company without going into too much detail. Now go ahead and try it yourself

---

ACTION POINTS

Using the steps described above, create your own Business description.

1. Write down your profession or industry, similar to the one which has been given in the example.

2. Using the keywords listed down previously for your Business, use these to compose a paragraph describing your company as given in the example.

3. Combine these two steps and use it to form the first part of your Business identity.

WHAT- Products and Services

The second part of the Business identity is the 'What'. The 'What' refers to the products or services which your company hopes to deliver to your customers. The main point of developing a Business is to be able to solve a particular problem and add value to the lives of your customers and you do this by either supplying a specific product or offering a specific service which solves the problem at hand.

Every product or service in the market is solving specific problems and the next section of the Business identity will examine the problems which your Business aims to solve. As the owner of the Business, it is imperative that you are fully aware of the products or services which your company will be offering.

Before looking at your products or services, it is important to understand the difference between a product and a service as many people tend to mix up the two. Understanding the difference between these two means that you are aware of which one you are offering.

The main difference between a product and a service is tangibility. A product can be touched, whereas a service is offered to you through labour. You cannot physically handle a service while you can handle a product. There are some Businesses that offer both of these so you have to be careful when differentiating between the two.

Example of such a Business which offers both products and service is an electronic retailer where they sell Televisions and offer an installation service with the television. When you purchase the television, you are buying a product, but paying for the installation is purchasing a service with the product. The same method applies to a restaurant where a food is cooked and served to you. They are offering products which are the different foods which they serve e.g. Hamburgers but the process of bringing the food and presenting it to you is a service which is being offered. A service will usually involve the use of labour. The process of selling the product to you will be done through a service. A checkout assistant at a till is offering you a service but the item you are buying is a product.

There are some companies who only offer services to their customers with no products attached.

E.g. a website designer will be offering a service as the sites being built cannot be touched or handled and an IT support company fixing computers are also offering services. However these companies can incorporate some element of products in their Business where an IT support company can sell virus checking software which can be handled and used by the customer. You must know whether you are supplying products, services or there is an element of both in your Business.

Moving on to the issue of being specific about the products or services which you aim to supply to your customers, you cannot attract customers if you do not clearly state the products or services which you are offering to them. Stating your products or services must be done in a clear and understandable way to every type of individual. One of the worst things that you can experience is to ask a Business owner what their company does and they are speaking to you, using terms and terminologies which you cannot understand.

When you are stating your products or services, you must break it down or state it in an understandable way so that the listener can grasp the value which it is likely to add to their lives.

The way in which you describe your products or services will depend on several factors such as the amount of products being offered, type of Business etc. Here are some examples of methods which you can adopt in describing your products / services:

Singular: This method refers to listing your products or services individually. This can be effective for Businesses that tend not to supply a lot of products. For example, if you are an IT support company, you could decide to list down the individual types of IT support services which you offer. These may not be a lot of services; hence you are able to state them as individuals. So you could state that you supply Virus removals, PC repairs, Security software installation etc. This approach will not be appropriate if you run a company that supplies numerous types of goods or services as this may be exhausting when trying to explain or list them to your customers. For example, if you run a convenience store which contains hundreds of products, you will not be describing each product to your customer but you can use another approach in listing the types of products which you offer.

Categories: Carrying on from the previous example of a convenience store, this approach will come into play for the convenience store. Using this approach to state the products and services which you supply as a company will apply if you supply different types of goods or services and you have decided to categorise them. Still using the example of a convenience store, the shop owner could decide that rather than list down all the products which are available in his store, he could just list down the types of products which he sells in different categories. For example, instead of listing down the different chocolate bars which he sells, he could decide to just have a category for "chocolate bars", another category for "newspapers", "magazines" and others. The point is that he is able to cover all the different products which his shop supplies by categorising them in a group based on the types of products which they are. The main problem with this type of approach is pricing. When you decide to categorise your products or services in a group, the prices of the individual products in each category may differ which means that you will have to break down the category even further. Another example of a Business that can use this approach is a fashion boutique which sells different types of accessories and clothing and may want to categorise them into the type of clothing or accessories which they are.

Packages: This is the third type of approach when describing the products and services which your company aims to offer to your customers. Packages is usually utilised by companies that supply services. For example, you could get a website designer that charges different prices for its services based on the customer needs.

Instead of taking an order from every individual customer and then figuring out the price to charge the customer, the easier way to approach this may be to offer packages to customers and each package will contain a different level of service. This can be done by listing down the packages with their respectivebenefits and prices. With this method, the price of the package will increase based on the benefits included in the package. This approach can also be used by companies who offer personal or Business services. For example, a Business or personal development coach can offer different types of coaching programmes where the client chooses a package depending on the benefits that come with each package e.g. number of sessions, amount of support etc.

Example

Here is an example of a 'package' approach where a website company sets out the packages which it offers its customers and the customers are able to choose from the packages based on their level of need:

Package One
Static Website
One Page
Domain Name Registration
Basic Logo Design

Package Two
Static Website
5 Pages
Domain Name Registration and 1 year Free Hosting
Logo Design

Package Three
Dynamic Website
5 Pages
Domain Name Registration and 1 Year Free Hosting
Logo Design
Corporate Identity and Business Card Design

Package Four
Dynamic Website
Up to 10 Pages
Domain Name Registration and 1 Year Free Hosting
Logo Design

Corporate Identity and Business Card Design
Content Management System
Social Media Plug-In

Package Five
Tailored Website Design
Unlimited Pages
Domain Name Registration and 1 Year Free Hosting
Logo Design
Corporate Identity and Business Card Design
Full Content Management (Training will be given)
Social Media Plug-In
E-Commerce

The example above shows how customers have been given a choice of package and each package clearly states the benefit. The advantages of this type of approach is that it allows you to easily create your financial statement and predict your future sales and costs based on the packages rather than charging individual customers based on their own personal needs. It also allows you to offer quick pricing to customers as they are able to check the packages first, see the price of each package or call in to check the price of the individual packages listed. Either way, it will make the pricing process for both you and your customers easier.

Whichever method you choose for listing down your products or services, you must make sure that it is one that suits your Business type and one which is understandable by you, your employees and customers.

ACTION POINTS

After learning the difference between a product and a service, it is now time for you to state your products and services and also choose the methods which you will use in describing them.

1. Grab a piece of paper and create a table with two columns. In one column, write down all the products which your company will be offering. In the other column, write down the services that your company will be offering.

2. After listing down the different products and services that you will be supplying, write down the methods which you will be using to describe your products or services by choosing one of the methods mentioned.

<u>WHY – What Problems are you solving?</u>

Still on the subject of creating your Business identity, the next aspect of your identity is to consider the reasons for choosing this Business idea. As mentioned earlier, a business must be solving a particular problem. Before setting up a Business, you must have spotted an opportunity or seen a problem that needed to be fixed. That is the main focus of this aspect of the Business identity.

Sometimes, people go into Business for the wrong reasons and end up quitting when they find out that the Business may not turn out as they expect. One of the most common example is where someone starts a Business, looking for a 'get rich quick' scheme and them realises that it may take time to build the Business and get some substantial return on investment, the individual may end up giving up, thinking that the idea did not work.

It is true that every Business must make money and a Business that doesn't make money becomes a hobby. But money should not be the sole reason for starting your Business. If you find yourself going into a Business just for the sole purpose of making money, you may find that you do not last long running that particular Business. The reason behind starting your Business must go beyond the money factor. As the Business owner,it is important to have a drive behind your Business idea as the same passion that you have will be projected to your employees, customers and other people who come in contact with your company.

Example

Have a look at Richard Branson (founder of the Virgin Group) as an example, he represents his brand wherever he goes, even to the point that he appears in most virgin adverts. You can sense that he has a drive and passion for what he does and he loves it.

One of the characteristics of great entrepreneurs is the simple ability to spot opportunities where others see a problem. It is important for you to keep your eyes open wherever you go as opportunities will present themselves in different ways and shapes. When you visit a shop and the customer service is poor, instead of complaining, why not use it as an opportunity to start a Business that can deliver a better service. When you visit the nail shop and you have to wait for a long time to be served due to high demand for the service, why not see that as an opportunity to open up an alternative nail shop because there is obviously a high demand in the area. The main point is that becoming an entrepreneur is based on the ability to spot opportunities where there may be problems and find ways of turning these opportunities into Business ventures.

Your Product or service must be solving a particular problem in the market place because this means that you are adding value to your customers. Customers would not pay for a product or service which they do not see the need for in the market place. It is important to stress the value which your product is adding to its customers through your various marketing avenues. Sometimes Business owners can focus so much on making money and building a business rather that stress the importance and value of their products and services. Customers buy into value and you must know what value you are adding sothat you can effectively project this.

As a Business owner, you must understand the problem which your products or services are solving as you will come across situations where you will be asked this question. A typical example is where you require investment and you approach investors for money, one of the questions which they will ask is the need for your products or services in the market and why you think that your customers will pay for them.

The 'Why' part is the overall Business identity as it states the reason for the existence of the product or services which you are supplying. Just like every human being wants to know what their purpose it so they can achieve the purpose, the same concept applies to your Business. You cannot determine the success of your Business if you are not sure about the reason for its existence and of the problem that it is solving.

Understanding the problems which you are solving will also allow you to keep up to date with any issues in the environment which could affect your Business as you will know where to focus your attention. For example, if your Business supplies websites for small Businesses, you will know that you need to keep a look out for latest technological changes such as DIY websites that allows new Businesses to create their own websites as this could cause a threat to your Business. Your Business may be aiming to provide professionally designed websites to small Business start ups as they may not be able to afford the expensive websites from large companies. Therefore, the problem which you are solving is the fact that you are providing professional websites for clients who are not able to afford high end prices from the large web design companies. Knowing this means that you are able to structure all your strategies to match your objectives and aims by making sure that the income which you make from your customers is enough to cover all your cost as a company.

These are just some of the importance of understanding why you are going into your new Business. Your purpose must be made clear both to you, your customers and anyone else that may be involved in your company.

ACTION POINTS

After understanding the importance of stating your reasons for getting involved in your Business, it is time to apply this to your idea. Write down the answers to the following questions in relation to your Business idea:

1. What is your reason for choosing this Business idea?

2. What problems will your product or service be solving?

WHERE – The location of your Company and area of coverage

Still discussing the issue of creating your Business identity, the next part of your identity is your 'Where'. This refers to the location of your company as well as the area of coverage for your goods or services.

You cannot give a description of your Business without mentioning the areas of operation which your Business covers. One of the aspects of a Business which many Business owners fail to pay enough attention to is the location of their Business and this causes a huge downfall to the Business even from the start. It is important to understand the fact that your Business location is very crucial to the success of your Business. Your Business location refers to the Business premises: the area you have decided to trade from.

Apart from your Business location, your customers would also want to know which areas are covered by your Business products and services and it is very important to make this clear as lack of clarity will mean that your customers will not know if you are able to deliver your service in their area. For example, you may be covering a particular city, country or your products may be available to customers worldwide. Your choice, in terms of coverage, will be based on certain factors such as resources available, type of Business etc. We will also be covering this in greater details in upcoming chapters.

This chapter is only focusing on the issue of your Business location as part of your Business identity. There is a whole chapter which is dedicated to finding your Business location and using your location as part of your Unique Selling Point.

WHEN – Times of Operation

As a Business, it is important for you to inform your customers of the times of operation. Many Business owners take this for granted and do not clearly define times of operation. This can also form part of your Business identity. Different types of Businesses will operate at different times and days. There are some Businesses that tend to operate at normal Business hours which are Monday to Friday between 9am-6pm while there are other Businesses that can decide to open 24hrs a day for 7 days a week.

For example, you will find that there are Businesses such as convenience storesthat will open later than other Businesses and they tend to also operate on a Sunday where most other Businesses are closed. There are also other Businesses that may offer their services 24 hours a day and 7 days a week and such Businesses are usually those which may be required in emergency such as a plumber, locksmith etc. There are several factors to consider when choosing your own Business operating hours. Consider the following factors:

Your Type of Customers: This is one of the main factors that can determine your opening hours as a Business.

When looking at opening hours in relation to your target market, one of the things which you will need to consider is your customers' lifestyle.

For example, a barber shop may decide to open till late on a Friday and Saturday in order to cater for the customers who work in the corporate world and would always want to come in on a Friday evening for a quick haircut before going out on the weekend. The same applies to a web designer who caters for small Businesses, there will be no reason to open on a Sunday or Saturday evening where most Businesses will not be operating and therefore would not be in need of the web services

Coffee shops have to open very early in the morning in order to cater for the workers who are travelling to work very early in the morning and the same applies to restaurants who serve breakfast to make sure that they open as early as possible in order to start serving their breakfast menu to the workers who tend to start work very early in the morning.

As a Business, the first step to take when choosing your operating times is to look at your target customers and examine when they will be available and the times when they are most likely to be buying your products or services.

Type Of Products or Services: The types of products and services which you offer will determine the times of operation which you will choose for your Business. There are different types of products and services that may be needed at several times. For example, if you are a plumber, your services could be needed at midnight if there is a pipe burst in a customer's house which could lead to flooding.

Similarly, if you are planning to open a dinner, you will need to consider a late opening and late closing time because your services will be in demand mostly in the evenings where customers would come in for evening meals and maybe lunch. Another typical example is a convenience store that sells everyday products. Owners will want to open as early as possible because they are products which customers will require at any time of the day and some convenience stores even open till about 11pm as they have to make sure that customers have access to their products at different hours of the day such as milk for breakfast, cooking products etc. You will need to evaluate your products or services and look at the times when they will be needed.

Location of Your Business: The issue of your Business location will come up several times in this book as it is a factor that determines a lot of decisions in your Business. Your opening times will also be affected by the location of your Business. For example, if you are operating from a city centre where most Businesses in the area close by a certain time, it will be quite unreasonable for you to still be opened after the other Businesses are closed as there is probably going to be no customers visiting the area.

Similarly, different countries and cities tend to have different operating times for the Businesses in the area. It Is therefore important for you to look at the trading hours for Businesses in your location before setting yours as this will normally indicate the times when customers are more likely to enquire about your product or services.

Your Method of Distribution: This is a factor that hasn't been mentioned in this book so far and will be examined in great detail in upcoming chapters. Your method of distribution refers to the way in which you have chosen to get your products to your customers, you could decide to use distributors, use a website for trading, or trade direct to your customers either through a shop or other types of premises.

The means which you have chosen to distribute your products or services will affect the times of operation. For example, an online fashion boutique could give their customers 24/7 access to their products through the website.

Using an online platform to sell your products or services means that your customers are able to place orders and the orders can be shipped to them at the agreed times. However, this type of service cannot work for a Business which trades from a shop front as there are restrictions on opening times and customers will probably not be walking into the shop after normal Business trading hours. Similarly, if you are a distributor who distributes your products and services to retailers, you could also have flexibility on trading hours as you are not facing the consumers directly and you can decide to work with the retailers to agree on times of delivery.

There are some methods of distribution that can be operated with minimal input and these are the ones that give you flexibility on trading hours and times when your customers can have access to your goods and services. An example is an e-commerce website where customers can order and pay for goods at any time and all that needs to be done is send out the ordered goods. With this platform your customers can have access to your products or services without being restricted by closing or opening times.

Type of premises: The type of premises which you have chosen to use for your Business will also have an impact on the times of operation. As you will find out in upcoming chapters where you will learn about the various types of Business premises, you can decide to trade from such premises as commercial offices, shop fronts, home based office etc. Your type of premises can affect your opening hours, for example, if you are working from home, you have more flexibility on the times when you can serve your customers as you are not restricted by laws and regulations regarding Business opening and closing times for shops.

With home based Businesses, you can choose your trading hours based around other commitments such as a full time job. With commercial offices, you can also choose to operate and serve your customers at times which suit you but this also depends on the opening and closing times for your office building. With retail shop fronts, different countries have their own laws and it is important for you to find out the laws regarding opening times for your own country or location if you plan to use a shop front as your Business premises

Apart from knowing your normal trading hours, the next issue to consider is when customers will have access to different aspects of your Business. When talking about the different aspects of your Business, this refers to the different types of operations that take place in your Business. For example, you could have a customer service, sales, technical and returns section of your Business.

Some Businesses have different times of operations for different aspects of their

Business, for example, some large retail stores use both shops and online platforms to distribute their products to their customers and even though their stores could close at certain times, customers would have access to their online platform where they could still order their products for delivery. You have to look at your Business and look at the different resources and sections which you will have and consider the times when your customers will have access to these different parts.

Another example is where you choose to give your customers access to your products or services 24 hours a day and 7 days a week but they may only have access to a customer advisor or staff member during normal Business hours when they can either walk into your premises or call your staff through the telephone. You have to look at the resources which are at your disposal and how many part of your company will be serving your customers, then you can determine the operating times for these different parts.

One of the easiest ways to determine the most suitable opening hours for your Business as a new start up is to open for as long as possible in your first month or so that you can explore the buying habits of your customers and this will allow you to set effective opening hours.

Another tip to consider is making sure that your operating times is clearly stated for your customers and this can be done either through your shop window, website or any other means by which you choose to relay information about your Business to your customers.

ACTION POINTS

After looking at the different factors that can affect your opening times, you can now make a decision on your Business opening hours. Write down the answer to the questions below in relation to your Business.

• What would be your opening hours

• If your Business has different departments that serve different customers, list
 down each department and write down their opening hours.

HOW – Method of Operation

The 'How' is the final part of your Business identity. As you have seen so far, the Business identity will give you a foundation for your Business which you can then go on and build upon. The 'How' of your Business refers to the 'mechanics' of the

Business. This refers to the process which drives your Business. This is the part of your Business identity where you have to go into further details and explain the processes involved in your Business operations.

As a Business owner, you have to make sure that you are aware of the processes which are involved in your Business. That is, from acquiring the materials used to produce your products or services to the point of distribution where your products or services actually get to the hands of your customers. Whether the Business only involves you, you have a partner or you plan to employ staff members from the start of your Business, it is important to be fully aware of the processes involved in your Business circle as the owner of the Business.

The methods of operation for your Business can be broken down into three stages:

1. Production Process

2. Method of Distribution

3. Product Delivery Roadmap

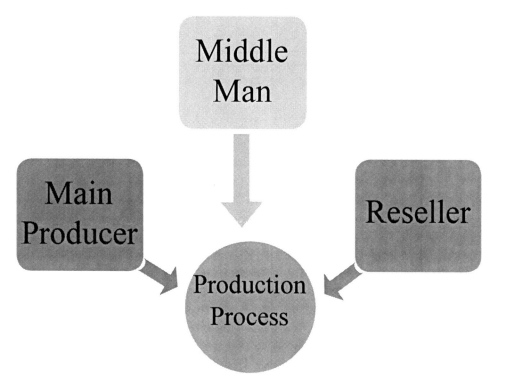

When I talk about your Production Process in this instance, I am referring to the ways you produce your products or services. Your production process here refers to the method which you plan to undertake in order to create the product or service that you are delivering to your customers. For example, an owner of a restaurant will have to buy the entire foodstuff needed to make all the food and then use the ingredients to prepare the variety of meals offered on the restaurant menu. This is what we refer to as the production process, where you are able to create your products or services.

Different types of Businesses will utilise different production processes and it is essential for you to know yours. There are three main methods that you can use in developing your products or services, they are:

Main Producer: Being the main producer refers to being the person who makes the product or creates the service from scratch. With this method, the idea belongs to you and you do not rely on anyone else to supply you with the products or services that you are supplying.

There are several examples of this; a restaurant will fall into this category where all the food is made from scratch at the premises to be served to the customers. A plumber will also fall into this category where he is the one who provides the service himself and he has the skills. This method will usually apply where you have the direct skills needed to provide the products or services which you are offering. Other types of services that may fall into this category are hair stylists, web designers etc. Even though we have mentioned web designers, some web design companies may not fall into this category. Some of them do not directly offer all the services which are offered by their company and they rely on third party providers of the service. A web designer or web design company will only fall into this category if they have the team in house who have the skills to provide all their services.

When it comes to this method, there are different ways which you can produce your own products or service. This will depend on several factors such as the type of products or services, the resources which you have at hand and several other factors. For example, a restaurant will still rely on supplies of the food stuff used to make all the food delivered to their customers and in the same light, a hair stylist will still depend on the distributors of hair products which she will use for clients' hair. Similarly, a company which creates its own beauty products has to purchase some raw materials which will be needed to make the products. This is the first way, which means that you are the one who makes the final product or service which is delivered to your customers but you still depend on some other providers to supply you with some elements which will be used in producing the final product or service.

The second way which you can produce the products or services yourself is by making it all from scratch. When we talk about making it all from scratch, this refers to a Business where you do not rely on other providers or suppliers to provide the elements that may be needed in delivering your final product or service to your customers. For example, offering life coaching services or counselling services means that you are the one who delivers the service to your clients and this is solely based on your skill and time and you do not have to depend on a third party in order to provide your services.

These are just examples of ways which you can produce your goods or services as the main producer.

Here are some of the advantages of this process:

• You are in control of the quality of your products or services which you are delivering to the clients.

• You can manage the turnover time for delivering the products or service to your clients as you are producing them directly.

• There is flexibility on the price which you can charge for your products or services as they are produced directly by you.

There are also some disadvantages such as:

• The cost is likely to be more than the other methods as you are in charge of producing the products or services and you will need to get all the materials needed to produce it.

• The process is likely to take longer to turnaround than the other methods as you are involved with the production and therefore you may have to go through some process before delivering the final product or service. For example, producing a hair cream may involve going through several due diligent processes in order to ensure quality and safety of the product.

Middle Man: With this method, you become a 'middle man' in offering the products or services to your customers. A 'middle man' refers to the production process which involves introducing a client to a service provider and getting paid a commission for it. With this type of production process, you are not producing the products but you are the one supplying it to the customers. This simply means that you are the link between the suppliers of the products itself and the buyer or customer.

There are two ways which this method can work:

• The first way is where you are in charge of the transaction. With this process, you are theone who ensures that the transaction between the main supplier and the customers go through smoothly. An example of this type or process can be found in an Estate Agency where the agency represents both the Landlord and the tenants and ensures that the transaction between both parties run smoothly by drawing up all the necessary documents, agreements and hands over the keys to the tenants.

With this process, you still have some work to do as the customer may not lay eyes on the main supplier but they trust that you are able to ensure that the transaction goes through smoothly and successfully. You will need to have a good knowledge of the product or service which you are involved in and ensure that the quality which is being supplied to the customer is a good one as you are representing the supplier.

• The second way to become a middle man is simply to introduce a supplier to a customer who is in need of the product and get a commission for it. An example of this can be a web design company that also enlists Company registration as one of its services which it offers but all it does is refer the clients to another company that actually supplies the web registration service. By doing this, the web design company gets a commission for referring the client without really doing anything and all the paperwork and any other process is carried out by the main supplier of the products or service.This type of process is very common among affiliate companies who basically refer you to suppliers or products or services and they get paid a commission fee for the referral. This is also common with comparison websites. In order to use this type of production process, you must first make an agreement with the suppliers that you would like to either find them customers or you would like to be an affiliate of their company and agree the right commission to be paid.

Here are some of the advantages of adopting this process:

- This tends to be a cheaper process than the first one as there may not be much resources needed to implement the process.

- This process will not take much of your time in supplying the product to the customer as all you are doing is referring and the supplier is the main producer of the goods or services.

- With this process, you may have different choices of suppliers, so you are able to offer the customers the best quality goods and services.

There are also some disadvantages in this process such as:

- As you are not the main producer of the goods or services, you are not in control of the quality control.

- Turnover time may cause problems as you are not directly in charge of this.

- Any problems which may arise on the suppliers end may have an impact on your company as you are the one representing both parties.

- There is not much flexibility in prices as you may only be entitled to a commission and not allowed to add any money on top of that which is demanded by the supplier.

Reseller: This is the third process that you can use in producing the goods or services which you intend on supplying to your customers. With this process, your main aim is to purchase the goods or services from the main supplier with the intention of reselling it to your customers. This is very common with convenience stores that buy different types of products at wholesale prices and sell them on to their customers by adding their own prices on top of it.

By becoming a reseller, you are buying the rights to resell a product or service on behalf of its original supplier. There are different types of reselling options that you can take on. Here are some of them:

Reselling a product or service under the original brand: This method is very common with convenience stores. This is basically buying goods from the suppliers in bulk or on a wholesale price and then supplying the products to your own customers with the original brand of the supplier.

With this type of process, you are only seen as the distributor of the product or service and any issues will be directed at the supplier. This type of process is very common as major suppliers tend to distribute their products through retail stores.

Here are some of the advantages that are associated with choosing this process:

- With this process, you are not liable for any damage or problems with the quality of the product or service as customers can contact the suppliers directly.

- This process will not take much of your time in supplying the product to the customer as all you are doing is referring and the supplier is the main producer of the goods or services.

- There is not much cost involved in the production process on your side as you are not the main producer of the goods or services.

There are also some disadvantages in this process such as:

- Even though you are not responsible for the quality of the products or services, the brand will still be associated with your company, so any negativity may still have an effect on your brand.

- You do not have any say in the production process and therefore have no say on the quality of the products.

Reselling a product or service, rebranded under your company's name: This is very similar to the first method however, with this reseller option, you buy a service or product from the main supplier and brand it under your own company name.

With this method, you would have developed a relationship with the main suppliers of the product or service to ensure that they are reliable and the goods or services supplied are of good quality. The reason is because when you rebrand the products or goods under your own company, any issues raised by your clients will be directed at you as they are not aware of the source of the product. As far as your customers are concerned, you are the one producing the goods or services.

This process is very common among companies that sub-contract their production to other companies. For example, a web design company could decide to offer email marketing as one of their services but they may not have the staff in house who can deliver the email marketing service. What they would have to do is to sub-contract this work out to a company that can provide the service, with the agreement that they will brand the service under their own company when presenting it to the customer and payment is made to the company which chooses to take on the sub-contract.

There are also several other examples of this. Companies that supply hair extensions tend to fall into this category where they buy the extensions from the original suppliers and some of these companies rebrand the product and supply it to the customers.

Here are some of the advantages of choosing this approach:

- You can manipulate the prices a bit more as you are now using your own brand and you can price the goods or services based on your pricing strategies.

- Your customers may trust this product more as it is your own brand.

- The cost of production will be low while still using your own brand.

There are also some disadvantages in this process such as:

- Selling the goods or services under your own brand means that you are certifying its quality which means that any problems with the products will automatically be assumed on your own brand.

- Any damaged products which you may have acquired and branded may go to waste if they are not sold to the customers.

After looking at each individual production process, you must bear in mind that it is possible for your company to make use of multiple processes for different products or services which you supply. For example, a web design company may choose to add on some extra products to its list of services which is subcontracted to another company.

You must know the different processes that apply to your different products or services.

ACTION POINTS

You have learnt the different types of production processes. It is now time to think about your own production process for your new Business. Make a list of all the products or services that you provide and list the production process that you will use for each of them next to it.

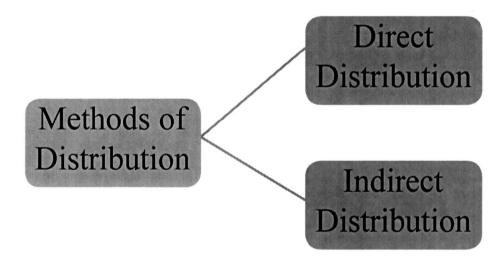

After looking at the production process, the next step is to look at how you plan to get your products or services to your customers. Distribution basically means the act of getting your products or services to your customers e.g. if you plan to open a store which sells beauty products all over the world, you must be able to define how you intend on getting the products to all your customers in the different countries.

When thinking about getting your products or services to your customers, you can think about it in two ways:

'You can either find an opportunity or create an opportunity'
A lady who wishes to own her own clothing brand can either decide to approach existing clothing shops to sell her designs for her or she can use the internet to market her designs herself directly to her customers. Approaching existing clothing shops means that she is looking for existing opportunities while using the internet to access her market directly means that she is creating an opportunity for herself. This is where the two types of distribution come into play.

The two types of distribution are direct and indirect distribution.

Direct Distribution Channel: Direct distribution occurs where you choose to sell your products directly to your customers without having to go through other companies or agencies. This means that there are no third parties involved in the distribution process that take ownerships of your products or services. This type of distribution has been made easier with the rapid growth of internet usage where customers are able to access your products or services quickly through the internet. This channel of distribution also cuts costs which could be incurred through the use of "middle men" or third parties. This is where creating opportunities comes in. You look for ways to access your customers directly.

With direct distribution, you will have more control over how your products or services are distributed to your customers. One of the main differences between the direct distribution method and indirect distribution method is the 'cost factor'. It will cost you less if you adopt an indirect distribution method than a direct one. With a direct distribution method, you are responsible for putting together the facilities or means of getting the products to your customers e.g. if you want to open a retail outlet, you will be responsible for acquiring the shop spaces needed and all the other equipments needed for the shop and this may cost quite a bit to set up whereas it might not cost as much in the process of an indirect distribution method.

With a direct distribution method, there are several ways in which your Business can get its products or services directly to the customers. This is known as a method of communication. The method you choose will depend on several factors such as your type of Business, your target market, your budget etc. Here are some of the communication methods you can use for your Business if you choose to go down the direct distribution route:

- E-Commerce – This type of communication is one where you do not have a personal contact with the customer when delivering the product or service to them. With this method of communication, the customer places their orders through a system such as your website etc. With E-commerce, there is an opportunity to be flexible with operating times for your Business where customers do not have to communicate directly with you during the distribution process. An example of companies that could use this method of communication could be an online fashion boutique where customers can order their products through the website.

• Retail Outlet – This is a method of communication where you choose to operate from a retail outlet e.g. operating from a shop. Examples are high street shops which sell clothes or food.

• Sales Team – This is where your business involves the process of persuading buyers to purchase your goods or services through the use of a sales team. With this method, your sales team have the task of generating sales from your customers and the customers have to place the orders either through the phone or in person. This can be used for your business if you intend on using cold-calling as one of your main marketing strategies for acquiring customers.

• Assisted Marketing Systems – With this method, your marketing is dependent on others but you are responsible for the distribution of your products or services. This method does not involve a 'middle man' when it comes to distributing your products or services and dealing with your customers, but you can make use of others to increase your brand awareness and marketing. Example of this method is E-bay or Gumtree, where you are able to offer your products or services to your customer base in different locations for a fee but you are in charge of the actual distribution.

There are certain businesses that can choose to use multiple communication methods for their distribution, e.g. there are some companies who choose to trade out of a retail outlet and also have an online platform and catalogue where customers can place orders e.g. big supermarkets such as Tesco in the UK.

Indirect Distribution: This is where you do not supply your products or services directly to your customers but intermediaries are involved in the distribution process. With this type of distribution, you do not have a great level of control. The indirect distribution method involves the use of 'middle men' such as agents, distributors, licensees, affiliates, franchisees and other routes. This type of distribution method may be appropriate for your business if you choose to distribute your products or services to customers in a wider location at a lower cost. This method of distribution tends to cost less to establish as mentioned before.

With the indirect method of distribution, you aim to reach the target market with the help of others such as resellers. These resellers either take ownership of selling your products or they can choose to sell your products on a consignment basis where they only pay you for products or services sold. You may want to focus on just producing your goods or services and want to outsource your selling or distribution to other companies or 'middle men'; this is where you choose to use indirect distribution.This method can help you reach a wider market while retaining your brand.

An example of a Business where indirect distribution will come into play is an author who writes a book and wishes to make it available in several countries; he might want to use platforms such as large distributers or bookshopswhich may pay him a royalty for each book sold. This will help him in distributing his books to a large market while he focuses on writing more books.

With the emergence of so many online platforms and websites where you can distribute your products, it is now easy for Businesses to go through the indirect route of distribution and get their products and services to a mass audience without having to pay a large sum of money.

When making a decision on your distribution methods, the three main factors to consider are the costs involved, the level of control which you will have over the distribution process and the coverage intended for your products and services. For your Business, it is important to consider how much you would like to invest in your distribution and also look at which areas you would like to be covered by your products and services. This will give you an idea on which method to go for.

For example, there is no point using an indirect distribution where you only need to target clients in your local area and you can operate from a simple office space. This may give you a lot of control over how your service is delivered. With the help of technology, direct and indirect channels of distribution have become quicker and easier.

Whichever method you choose to use for your distribution, you can be sure that it will be done successfully as long as you consider the factors stated above. It is your decision whether to sell directly to your customers or you would prefer to sell to companies who can then resell your products or even use both. When making the decisions, consider which methods will make the most out of your products or services and give you a good profit margin.

ACTION POINTS

After learning about the different methods of distribution, hopefully you are able to make a decision regarding the best distribution method(s) for your Business. Write a paragraph explaining the type of distribution which you have chosen for your products or services and why. Give an explanation of the method which you have chosen.

If you have chosen both types of distribution, write down how you will do this

---

Once you have established your production process and you have also defined your distribution method, the next step is to create a product delivery roadmap for your Business. The product delivery roadmap connects the two stages together. Your roadmap can be compared to a car satellite navigation system.

It contains the process that takes place from the point of contact with a potential customer to the point where the product or service is delivered to your customer. Your roadmap will state the step by step process that is involved in delivering your product or service to each customer from the point where a customer calls you to the point when they receive the service or products from you and you can even go further by stating any after-care service that will be offered to the customer.

Every Business will have a different type of product delivery roadmap, depending on several factors such as size of Business, types of products and services, production process, method of distribution etc.

You may even find that there is a different delivery roadmap for different products or services that you offer.

Example

Let's take a look at an example of a product delivery roadmap for a plumber:

1. The customer calls the plumber and reports a fault

2. Plumber fills in enquiry form to make note of service needed and address of customer

3. Plumber gathers the right tools, gets in the van and sets off to the client's address

4. The plumber gets to the address, has a look at the problem

5. Plumber presents client with quote

6. If any parts are needed, then the plumber orders the parts.

7. Plumber fixes the problem

8. Client Pays plumber

9. Plumber gives client receipt

10. Plumber presents client with a 'job sheet' to sign

This is just a simple example of a product delivery roadmap to give you an idea. Developing a good product delivery roadmap will help create a process which can be used by anyone involved in the Business. It also ensures that new employees can be easily integrated into the Business.

Before you can develop a roadmap for your Business, you must first create the different stages needed and determine the steps that you would like to be taken with every customer. The roadmap will be different for different types of Businesses, for example, the roadmap for a large supermarket will be different from that of a plumber. Now it's time to have a go and create your own roadmap.

<u>ACTION POINTS</u>

You have already chosen your production process and your methods of distribution; therefore creating your roadmap should not be too hard.

Using a flow chart, create a product delivery roadmap for your Business. If you find that different products require different roadmaps, create all the roadmaps for each product or service that you have.

STEP 3

CHECK THE VIABILITY OF YOUR IDEA

"Everyone who's ever taken a shower has an idea. It's the person who gets out of the shower, dries off and does something about it who makes a difference"

NOLAN BUSHNELL

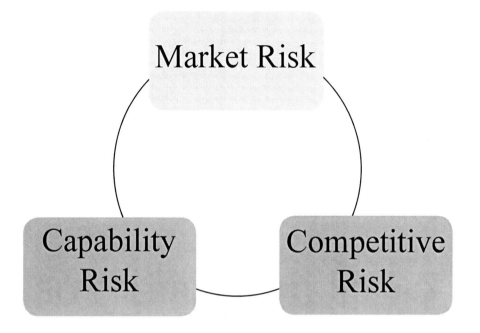

Once you have defined your Business identity, the next step is to measure the viability of your idea. Measuring the viability of your idea simply means that you are checking whether your idea will work or not. One of the biggest mistakes you can make is to come up with an idea, invest your money towards the idea and then find out that the idea does not work or there is no need for the product or service in the market. It is therefore important to conduct some research before taking the next steps towards turning your idea into a reality.

Measuring the viability of your idea must be done through careful research especially when you are bringing out a product which doesn't currently exist in the market. When you want to start a Business which already exists or get involved in a popular industry, it is easier to judge the viability of the idea as there is already a demand for the product.

Example

If you wanted to start an Estates Agency; with the amount of competition in the market and the demand for properties, all you need to worry about is how to stand out from your competitors and gain a share of the market. Whereas if you were to develop a new mobile app that has never existed before, you would not be sure of how users would react to it and you may need to carry out extensive research before creating the full app.

In order to measure the viability of your idea, I always recommend using the 'New Business Assessment Risk'. If you look at investors and other people who regularly explore Business ideas to see their viabilities, they will tell you that they do not always get it right and there are some Businesses which they have written off, which end up becoming highly successful by other investors. An example of this can be found on the British television show (The Dragons Den) which shows investors looking for viable Business ideas to invest in. You will find that there are some Business ideas which they reject due to their inability to spot the opportunity for the product or service and some of these Businesses go on to become successful anyway. This is due to the owner of the Business believing in the idea and carrying out sufficient research to be convinced enough to follow the idea through, despite opposition from the Business experts.

In other words, as an aspiring entrepreneur, you must be able to judge the viability of your idea before you approach anyone else with the idea as you will always have different people giving you different opinions based on their own experience or knowledge with regards to the idea and its industry. There is no ultimate guarantee that a Business idea will always go as planned but you can always ensure that you carry out some checks which will help you to identify the weaknesses and strengths of your idea.

The 'New Business Assessment Risk' refers to those factors that can be used to measure the sustainability and viability of your Business idea and this is a format which can be applied to any idea which you may come up with.
The most important thing when carrying out the new business assessment risk is to be honest with yourself as the owner of the Business. The aim of the process is not to put you off your idea. The main purpose is to give you a reality of your idea and its potential market. It allows you to ensure that the idea is worth pursuing and can help reduce the risk of losing time and money on an idea which may not work. The assessment also helps you to look at areas which may need changing in order to improve the concept.

The new Business assessment risk is broken down into three categories:

1. Market Risk

2. Competitive Risk

3. Capability Risk

These three risks will enable you to find out your strengths and weaknesses both as an individual and as a Business owner. Each category will include some questions which you have to answer as the prospective Business owner.

In order to effectively measure the outcome of these risks, the best way to carry out the research is to do it with people who you can trust with your Business idea in order to avoid leaking your idea to someone who might potentially steal it. The aim of the assessment is to get a YES to all the questions which are being asked and also to modify the areas where there is a NO in order to improve it.

Now let's examine each category:

MARKET RISK

The first assessment looks at the market which you are about to enter. Your first step is to find out if there is actually a demand for your products or services in your marketplace. With the market risk, there are two main questions which you will need to ask yourself:

Is there a demand from customers for your Products/ Services?: One of the most common mistakes that you can make is to think that 'Just because a particular skill comes easily to you, then everyone should be able to do the same thing' and this means that no one would really be in need of the service or product being offered. You must understand that your focus should be on finding a problem and fixing the problem and this means that as long as you are solving a particular problem, there should be someone or a group of people who are in need of your product or services.

Demand for your products or services simply mean that people are in need of the products or services that you are supplying. There is no point starting a Business when there is no one who wants the goods or services which you are offering. There are several ways of finding this out. You can either use a questionnaire, interview potential customers, conduct secondary research such as checking out market trends, industry analysis or using other avenues that are available to you. The main point is to speak to people you can trust with your Business idea and find out if there is a need in the market for your product.

Your customers are the lifeblood of your Business and therefore your focus should firstly be to find out if there is a demand from customers for your products or services. Another way to carry out a research is to have a focus group where you can gather a number of trusted individuals who can give you their views on your product or service and you can use this to gain a different perspective to your

Business idea.

You will find that positivity and optimism tends to blind people into pursuing a Businessideawhichisnotrequiredinthemarketplaceandhencehasashortlifespan.

Whatever method of research you choose to use, you must make sure that you are targeting your right audience and you are also getting as much information as possible from the research participants.

<u>Are people willing to pay for your solution to the Problem?</u>: After looking at the need for your product or services in the market, the next issue which you need to discuss is whether people are ready to pay for your products or services. It is important to understand that there is a difference between finding a market for your products or services and also finding a customer base that are willing to pay. Without a good cash flow in your Business, it will not last long at all, therefore you must make sure that you've got a product or services which people are looking for and most importantly, people are willing to pay for.

"Doing something you love without getting paid for it counts as a hobby"

The best way to carry out this research is also to use similar methods discussed in the first question. It is important to get out there and find out from the target market whether they have the money which you are requesting for your products or services or whether they are willing to pay for your products or services at all.

Example
If you are producing hair products for young girls aged between 15 and 18, you will be aware of the affordability of that age group and ensure that the price which you are charging is realistic.

You must therefore ensure that you carry out adequate research in order to find out whether people are going to pay for your products or services which you have to offer. Remember, just because there is the gap in the market doesn't mean that people will be willing to pay for it.

When exploring the willingness of your market to pay for your products or services, you must also consider the alternatives which exist in the market. If you are bringing a product to the market and there is an alternative which people can get that will offer the same benefits but they can get for free, this could create a problem for you. This is why it is essential to carry out a detailed competitive research before you enter any market.

Example

If you are a web designer targeting Business Start-ups at universities, you may find out that there may not be enough money in their start-up budget to cover the cost of the website design and they may prefer to use free website templates and wizards to create their own websites at the start-up phase. Therefore you must be aware of the alternatives which can act as a barrier for getting paid for your products or services.

These are the questions which encompass the market risk assessment. Every time you come across any idea at all, these are the two questions which you must first ask yourself.

ACTION POINTS

After looking at the first category of the new Business assessment, the next is to apply the questions to your own idea.

Ask yourself the following questions:

- Is there a demand from customers for my products / services?
- Are people willing to pay for my solution to the problem?

Rate your answers between 1 and 5. (1 = Yes, Very Sure,   5 = No, Not Sure)

Once you have given your answer, conduct a research using the methods given to find out the results from your target market.

COMPETITIVE RISK

Still on the subject of assessing the viability of your Business idea, the second risk assessment which needs to be carried out is the Competitive Risk. The competitive risk involves carrying out a research into your competitive market in order to explore your ability to compete in your new industry and market.

In further chapters, you will find out how to define your Unique Selling Point and how to explore your competitors but the main focus of this section is to give you a template for examining your ideas in relation to your competitors.

When you have a Business idea, one of the first issues that you have to start looking at are the products or services which are similar to yours in the market and look at ways in which you can differentiate yourself from these competitors.

With the competitive risk analysis, there are also two questions which you must ask yourself:

Can your Business Survive Competition? As a new Business owner, you may face competition from either direct or indirect competitors. The level of competition that you will face will depend on the factors which you will find out later in this book. It is therefore important for you to put some strategies in place to ensure that you are able to survive competition in your new market.

The first question which you need to examine in the competitive risk assessment is your ability to survive the competition you may face with your new Business and the products and services which it is bringing into the market place.

It is crucial that you explore the competitive environment in your new market. You may find yourself in a highly saturated market or one where competition is scare but the key is to know the level of competition which you are likely to face in your new Business in order to plan and develop a clear strategy which will allow you to survive the competition.

Just imagine lions in the wild that have to compete in order to hunt for the same food. Each lion will have to develop tactics which would allow it to get to the prey first before its competition and the same principle applies to you as a new Business owner. You need to start thinking about ways to survive the threat from existing competitors.

When you are confidently able to answer a YES to this question, then you can go on to the next question in the competitive risk.

Are your products/services differentiated from your competitors? This question deals with the issue of defining your unique identity as a Business. You have already created an identity for your Business but you must also ensure that your products or services have a unique selling point which will separate them from your competitors.

Just like every individual wants to be unique and stand out, it is important for your Business to be able to stand out in your market.

Examine the other products or services in the industry which you are about to enter and ask yourself:

What would make my customers choose my products or services over my competitors?

Once you are able to answer this, you can be confident that you will use this in your promotion, marketing and advertising in order to gain market share.

Example

In the computer tablet market, there are so many competitors that every company competing in the market must always add an innovative feature to their tablet and this will be portrayed in the advertising and promotion.

Apple is one of those companies who always ensure that it adds innovative features to its products which makes it stand out from its competitors and attract the customers to its new products. Such features were the 'Siri' voice recognition software, the retina display etc.

Differentiation is a process that ensures that you stay ahead of your competitors at all times, you must therefore ensure that you are constantly innovating your products or services.

If you find yourself struggling to answer a resounding YES to these questions, you will learn different ways of differentiating yourself in further chapters.

ACTION POINTS

Apply the same principle from the first category to the Competitive risk. Answer the following questions in relation to your Business idea:

• Can my Business survive competition?
• Are my products or services differentiated from my competitors?

Rate your answers between 1 to 5 (1 = Yes, Very Sure, 5 = No, Not Sure)

Once you have given your answer, conduct a research using the methods given to find out the results from your target market.

CAPABILITY RISK

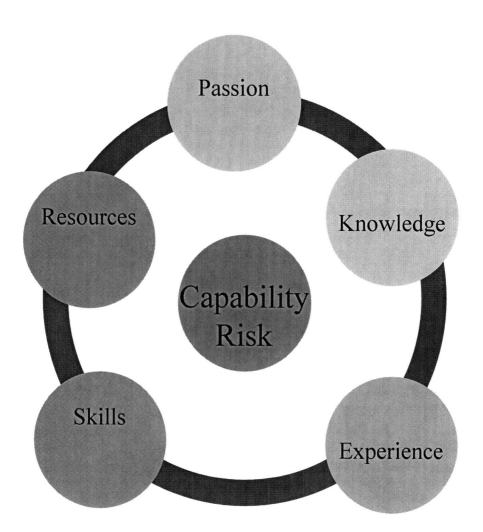

As you will find out later in this book, one of the most effective means of advertising is 'Word of Mouth'. Your Business can either become very successful through word of mouth advertising or it can be destroyed through the same means. A typical example of this is the 'Facebook' social media platform which has grown to nearly 1 billion users at this point in time and is still rapidly increasing and this is mainly due to word of mouth promotion.

Still looking at the issue of assessing the viability of your Business idea, the third risk which needs to be examined is the **Capability Risk**. As the name suggests, the capability risk refers to your ability to deliver your marketing promises to your customers. One of the biggest mistakes which a new Business can make is to 'over promise' and 'under deliver'. This basically means that you must ensure as a new Business owner that you do not promise to deliver a product or service to your customers which you do not have the capability to deliver.

This will only result in creating a bad reputation for your company among your potential customers right from the start and you will end up having to work even harder in order to convince your customers about the quality of your product or service.

The question which you need to ask yourself in this third section is this:

"Do I have the capability to deliver the product or service which I have decided to offer?"

It is important for you as an aspiring Business owner to look at the resources which you need in order to run the Business and also examine that which you currently possess as this will show you what you are lacking and guide you in assessing yourself using this third criterion.

As the Business owner, you have the responsibility of ensuring that the customer gets the products or services which your company promises to deliver and therefore, before starting off your new Business ensure that all the necessary resources are in place.

Your capability to deliver the products and services successfully to your customers can be measured by answering these five questions:

• **Passion:** How passionate are you about your Business idea?

• **Knowledge:** What qualifications do you have in the industry and how knowledgeable are you about your new Business Industry and market?

• **Experience:** Do you have any previous experience in the industry?

• **Skills:** Do you have the required skills to deliver the products or services promised?

• **Resources:** Do you have the required resources needed to produce and deliver your products or services?

Now let's explore each one in order to find out how it applies to your own Business idea:

Passion

At the start of this book, I mentioned the importance of starting a Business which you are passionate about and also looked at the different ways of finding your passion. As mentioned earlier, most successful Businesses are run by passionate Business owners as this is an important ingredient in delivering a top service to your customers.

Top companies all over the world are owned by people who are passionate about what they do and are constantly looking for innovative ways of delivering quality products and services to their customers. As well as being driven by passion as the Business owner. It is also important to have a team that is passionate about the products or services which they are delivering.

Example

Take a look at the late Steve Jobs of Apple, Richard Branson or Virgin, Bill Gates of Microsoft, Mark Zuckerberg of Facebook etc. These are all individuals who have been able to build multibillion pound companies and one of the traits that they all share is their passion for their products and services.

They are always looking for new ways to innovate and offer added benefits to their products hence they all have a broad market. This shows the importance of being passionate.

As the Business owner, opportunities will arise where you will either pitch your Business idea to potential customers, investors or anyone else who may be interested in your Business. You must understand that:

Once your customers buy into you as a person, they will be more interested in buying your product or services

When you are passionate about your products or services, it will be easier to talk about it or sell your idea to the listener. Your passion can be projected through your enthusiasm; the way you describe your Business and even your body language can give an idea of how passionate you are about your idea when you are describing it.

Passion gets you through the difficult times of your start-up. Once you are passionate about your idea, this will give you an incentive to push harder to create a successful Business. As the owner of the Business, if you create a Business which is not driven by passion, it may reflect on your company as a whole including your staff members.

All you need to do is simply ask yourself this question:

How passionate am I about this Business idea?

When you can confidently answer a YES to this question, then you have passed the first assessment from the capability risk assessment.

ACTION POINTS

After looking at the importance of passion in any Business, measure how passionate you are about your new idea.

Ask yourself the following question:

• How passionate am I about my Business idea?

Rate your answers between 1 to 5 (1 = Yes, Very Passionate,   5 = No, Not passionate at all)

Knowledge

Knowledge is crucial to the success of any Business. You cannot deliver quality services or run a successful Business when you don't have the right 'know-how'. When talking about knowledge in terms of a Business start-up, this can be divided into different types:

• Knowledge of the industry: As an aspiring Business owner, it is important for you to have adequate knowledge of your industry. You must keep up to date with the latest developments within the industry and any laws and regulations which may affect your industry. For example, if you are starting a Business in the fashion industry, you must be aware of the latest trends and colours that may be 'in fashion' at any particular time.

It is important as a Business owner to be able to project adequate knowledge of your industry to your customers as well as this helps increase your credibility and build trust. There are several ways which you can develop your knowledge about your industry. One of the quickest and easiest ways is to use the internet. With the vast amount of information available through the internet, it has made it possible to lay hands on any type of information needed.

There are also several books available to read on different industries which can be used to increase your knowledge base on your chosen industry. Having the right skills is not good enough in becoming a successful Business owner, it is essential that you have adequate knowledge about your industry. There are other ways to keep up to date with your industry such as listening to the news, reading magazines, newspapers etc that are focused on your industry.

• Knowledge of your products / Services: It goes without saying that you need to have adequate knowledge of the products or services that you are planning to supply to your customers. You must be able to demonstrate your expertise in your profession.

Your customers would want to be assured and made confident that you have the right knowledge about the product or service that you are supplying.

Example

An Accountant has to be able to provide the right accountancy service and also give advice to his clients regarding their accountancy needs. In the same light, a pharmacist must be able to prescribe the right medicine to the customers and also give advice on the right medicine to use for different problems.

It is important for you to keep up to date with any laws, regulations or changes that may affect the products or services that you are supplying as your clients should be able to approach you for advice regarding them.

• <u>Knowledge of your Target Market:</u> While discussing the subject of having adequate knowledge, it is important to mention that you must have adequate knowledge of your target market. You must keep in touch with your customers' needs and their lifestyle.

In order for you to offer the best service to your customers, it is important to know enough facts about them and understand their needs. Before you start your Business, it is important for you to find out enough facts about your target market such as their disposable income, spending habits etc. these types of information will enable you to effectively plan your marketing strategy.

• <u>Knowledge of 'How to run a Business':</u> It is not good enough to merely know about your products or services and your chosen industry, it is also essential that you know about the 'ins and outs' of running a Business. There are several resources both online and offline that gives you tips and advice on how to start up your own Business and you must ensure that you take advantage of these.

Apart from available free advice, it is also important to have a good coach or mentor to guide you in starting your own Business. You must be willing to learn and improve your knowledge in terms of running your Business. This will help develop important skills as a Business owner. There are also training events, seminars and workshops that will aid you, giving you the tools which will guide you in successfully starting your new Business.

• <u>Essential Qualifications needed:</u> There are some professions that require a certain qualification before you can start trading. For example, you may need to complete your ACCA or ACA to become a qualified accountant. It is important for you to be aware of any qualifications which are needed to trade in your profession.

There are also other governing bodies or organisations that you may join to build the credibility of your company among your customers or give you a competitive advantage in your market. It is therefore important for you to know these certifications that may be needed to join these bodies. These governing bodies are charged with the task of regulating the laws regarding fair trading in certain industries and therefore joining these bodies will assure your customers that you are more likely to trade according to the laws and right standards.

The governing bodies will depend on your chosen industry and it is important for you to find out which one applies to your industry.
These are just some of the areas you may need to acquire knowledge of as a new Business owner and it is important for you to know which ones you are missing

and look for ways to gain them. This will only help you increase your capability as a Business owner.

ACTION POINTS

The next step after looking at the importance of adequate knowledge in a Business is to measure how knowledgeable you are in terms of your Business idea.

Grab a piece of paper and list down the following types of knowledge:

• Knowledge of your Industry
• Knowledge of your products / services
• Knowledge of your target market
• Knowledge of 'how to run a Business'
• Essential qualifications needed

Next to each type of knowledge, rate yourself between 1 to 5 (1 = Very knowledgeable   5 = Not knowledgeable)

The aim is to know which areas you are strongest and which areas need improving.

Experience

When looking at your capability to start a successful Business, another factor to consider is the amount of experience which you have in your chosen field. Even though many will argue this point, practical experience is one of the necessities in starting a successful Business. You must have some experience in the industry which you are about to enter.

Nowadays with the lack of employment and loss of jobs, many people are starting Businesses without a good level of experience. Gaining sufficient experience in your industry is essential as it increases your knowledge base and it also gives you essential skills that you may not gain on your own. Where there is no opportunity to gain a practical experience, many people fill this gap by gaining some knowledge through avenues such as books, seminars, mentorship etc.

When transitioning from full time employment to owning your own Business, you may have already gained the necessary experience if you decide to operate in the same industry but it's up to you to find out the various ways to gain the experience needed to successfully run your own Business. Lack of experience will always be obvious once you start trading and this will be most evident if your company delivers a service, rather than a product.

Example

If you decide to open a massage parlour, you may know the theory side of giving a good massage, but lack of practical experience in the industry means that you will not be able to have the essential skills and knowledge needed to successfully run a massage Business.

When it comes to your capability risk, it is important to note that your experience in the particular industry which you have chosen can help you deliver a better service to your customers. This is evident in such as areas where the Businesses use their experience in the field as a tool for attracting new customers.

Example

Where you find a number of Estate agents on the same road, one of them may mention the fact that they have been in Business for 30 years in order to prove their capability and experience in the industry.

There are some Businesses which require a certain level of experience before you can engage in the industry. For example, in order to own your own Solicitors firm, you may need to have worked for another firm for a minimum of three years. You will need to know about every requirement that you may face in terms of experience as you enter your new industry. This may be applicable, particularly to companies that are under a governing body which ensures that there is fair trading and all the companies in the industry can deliver products or services that are according to the general standard.

It is important to ensure that you do find a way of gaining the right level of experience that will enable you to deliver the best service to your customers. There are several ways that you can gain the experience needed in your industry. one of the most common ways is to gain full time employment in the desired industry, e.g. If you want to own an Estate agents, then you will need to work for an existing Estates agents in order to learn the trade and gain the required knowledge and acquire the skills needed.

The second way is to look for an internship or voluntary work with the aim of gaining the experience, even if it means that you do not get paid while doing it.

Where there is low level of employment, many turn to internships as an alternative. There are also some courses of certifications that will offer you practical work experience as part of the course which means that you may not need to seek another work experience after you have taken the course. This will depend on the type of profession that you are taking on.

When looking at your capability risk in terms of your experience, it is important to ask yourself the honest question of:

"Am I experienced enough to be able to deliver the product/service promised effectively?"

If you can confidently answer a YES to this question, then this will give you the confidence needed to pursue your idea further. This is the third step in measuring your capability risk.

ACTION POINTS

The next step is to measure your level of experience. You have already learnt the different ways of gaining the right experience for your field. In order to measure your experience, answer the following question:

• How experienced are you in your industry?

Rate your answer between 1-5 (1 = Very experienced, 5 = Not experienced at all) Also ask yourself the following question:

• What can I do to gain more experience in my field?

List the different options.

Skills

The fourth question which you need to ask yourself when measuring your capability risk is:

"Do I have the skills required in running this Business?"

Skills are different from knowledge as they are the more practical. Whereas knowledge comes in the form of information, skills are gained through either having a practical experience or some skills are developed naturally.

Different types of Businesses require different sets of skills in order to run them. For example, one of the most important skills that any Business owner must have is the ability to sell. Whatever type of Business you are running, you must be able to sell yourself and also sell your products or services to anyone who may be interested. Other skills which may be general to every business owner include networking skills, communication skills etc. there are also other personal skills which you need to have when you are starting off such as organisational skills, computer skills, time management skills, leadership skills, administration etc. These are some of the general skills which you need in order to run your own Business.

Apart from these general skills, there are some businesses that require specific types of skills such as public speaking skills, confidence skills etc. These skills will depend on your type of profession and the types of tasks which you will be dealing with on a daily basis.

Example

If you are a keynote speaker, you will know that a 'must-have' skill is good communication, confidence and public speaking skills. An accountant will definitely need some special skills such as book keeping, organisational, time management etc. In the same light, a website designer will need to have advanced computer skills where he is able to use certain software to build the websites or use certain programming languages. You must know the specialist skills that are needed for your profession.

There are certain skills which can only be developed from experience, especially where they are special skills which are tailored to your profession. For example, book keeping skills for an accountant can only be learnt through the experience of taking on the practical role. An accountant can be taught the theory aspect of book keeping, but it can never be the same as having the practical experience which will help develop the skills.

As previously mentioned, there are some skills which can be adopted naturally without any major experience in the field. For example, you can be naturally confident and this can help you in selling yourself or your product or service. You may find that you are naturally good at planning, time management or organisation and these can also be used to your advantage in your new Business.

There are specialist skills that cannot be developed naturally and these need to be gained through practical experience of practical training. For example, you may need to improve your computer skills in order to run your own Business and this may mean that you need to attend a computer training course which can take you through the practical training that will impart these skills in you.

You need to look at the skills which you possess and look at the ones that can be used in your Business and also look at those skills which you require in your Business and how to attain them. The right skills are very essential as a Business owner and must not be taken for granted. They can either help build your Business or a lack of them can destroy your new Business. Having the right skills will give you more confidence in terms of your capability as a Business owner in your profession.

ACTION POINTS

1. On a piece of paper, make a list of every skill which is essential for building a successful Business in your industry. Different examples of skills have already been given to you.

2. Next to each skill, place a tick next to the ones which you already possess.

3. Next to the skills which you don't currently possess, list different ways of gaining the relevant skills.

Resources

The last factor to consider when looking at the capability risk is the resources that you have at your disposal to use for your Business idea. When starting a Business, most people automatically think that the only resource needed is money. It is true that money can get you the other resources needed to start up your company but it is important for you to still understand that resources are needed as you may be able to acquire them without the need to pay for them. Here are some of the resources that you may need for your new Business:

Finances: Money is the first resource that comes to mind when most people think about running their own Business. This is one of the main resources that are needed to start a Business. A whole chapter of this book has been dedicated to the issue of financing your Business as it is important to ensure that you are able to access the finance needed to start-up. One of my favourite quotes is:

"Without money, the dream dies"

As a new Business owner, you will need to have some level of finance in order to fund your new start-up and this can also help you in delivering your products or services. Without the right level of financing for your new Business, you will not be able to progress. Therefore it is important to understand and ensure that you know how much is needed to start up your Business.

Manpower: The amount of manpower that you need for your new Business will depend on the type of Business you are starting up. There are some types of Businesses that can be started by a single individual while others require the recruitment of staff right from the start or forming a partnership.

Example

You may want to start a photography company and use your photography skills. This will only require your input at the start and you can then expand it in the future by bringing other photographers on board.

There are however examples of Businesses that do need extra manpower from the start, for example if you are opening a restaurant, you may require waiting staff to deal with the customers while you either manage the restaurant or cook the food in the kitchen.

These are just some of the examples of different types of manpower that can be required in your Business. This is a factor that will be tailored to our Business and it is important for you to know the amount of manpower which is essential to your start up and look for ways of acquiring these hands on board.

Having examined the issue of getting the right skills to run your Business, this ties in perfectly with the issue of having adequate manpower to run the Business. Look at the skills which are needed to run your Business effectively, examine the skills which you have and this will help you define which types of manpower is needed on board from the start. However amount of manpower you choose to utilise in your new Business, the most important thing is to ensure that you are not under-delivering to your customers.

Equipments: It is important to know the equipments you need in order to run your Business. The equipments will aid you in delivering your products or services effectively to your customers. Every business will require different types of equipment and it is up to you to find out which equipments are needed to start your own Business.

Example

The tools needed by a plumber will be different from those needed by an electrician or a photographer. There are some equipments that will be general to every profession such as a laptop, office accessories etc. There are also other equipments which will be unique to your profession and you must ensure that you have these, for example, a photographer must ensure that he has a good camera in order to deliver the right quality photographs to clients.

Your equipments are also part of your total resources for your new Business and ensuring that you have the right equipments will aid your capability in delivering the right service to your customers.

Premises: Your premises could also count as part of your resources needed to effectively start your Business. There are different types of premises and you will learn about the different types in greater details in further chapters. Whether you decide to trade from a home office, a shop front, a factory or a workshop, you will require some type premises to run your Business and it is important to understand which type of premises is most suitable for your Business. There are some Businesses that can trade from home while others will require external premises from the outset.

For example, a hair stylist should have a premise where they can deliver the service to their clients, except if they are mobile stylists. Acquiring the right premises also aids your capability to provide the right service to your clients.

After looking at the three different categories of risks that are associated with measuring the viability of your Business idea, the next step is to ask the questions which are associated with each risk and genuinely answer each question. If you have a confident YES for each one, then you can be sure that you have a winning idea, but if you do not, then you need to re-examine your idea using the concerned category. As you proceed through this book, you will learn how to modify your idea to become viable.

ACTION POINTS

Resources are very essential to making a good start to your Business.

• Write down all the resources that you require for your new Business.

• Next to each resource, place a tick next to each one that you already possess

• Next to the ones which you do not, write down the cost involved in possessing it and list down the different ways you can acquire it.

• At the end of the task, calculate how much you need to spend to get the resources needed to set up your new Business.

STEP 4

CREATE YOUR LONG / SHORT TERM GOALS

"Without goals, and plans to reach them, you are like a ship that has set sail with no destination."

FITZHUGH DODSON

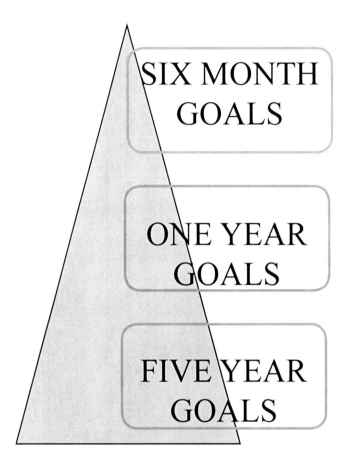

I tend to see goals as destinations. As a Business owner, you must get used to the idea of setting yourself goals or target and working towards them. At the start of your Business, you must establish your short term and long term goals or vision for your company. Creating your long term vision simply means that you have a picture of where you would like your company to be in the next 5 – 10 years. You must learn to work backwards. Set your goals and start working towards achieving them.

Every step that you take or every plan that you make in your company must always point towards your short or long term goals of the company. It is said that it takes the average Business up to 5 years to make a profit. It is however important to ensure that you know where you are going with your Business, even if you may not be turning over a profit in the first few years due to various expenses.

Here is an analogy that can emphasise the importance of setting long and short term goals:

Imagine driving along in your car, it is raining and you spot a friend at the bus stop waiting for a bus. You want to help your friend by giving him a lift to where he is going. You stop to ask him where he is headed so you can help him along the way.

When you ask him for his destination, he tells you that he doesn't have one. What would you think?

Then you ask him what bus he is waiting for and he also tells you that he's not sure. What would you think?

You would probably think that he is crazy and he is wasting his time at the bus stop as he wouldn't even know if the right bus drives past him.

This is what happens when you embark on your entrepreneurial journey without setting a clear destination for your Business. You cannot plan without having a goal.

Another analogy that best describes the notion of goal setting for your Business is building a house. When you want to build a house, you would have a picture of what you want the finished house to resemble in your mind. How many storeys you want the house to be, a rough size of the house or even the colour of the house etc. After you have created a clear vision of your house, then you can approach your Architect who can help plan your idea and draw it out so you can see the little details. After you have established the full picture in your mind, you can then start laying the foundation and then start laying one brick at a time which will allow you to bring your vision to a reality.

The same principle applies to owning a Business, you must first have the picture of the Business in the future and understand where you want to go as a Business owner and this will allow you to know the right steps to take and allow you to know which type of 'bricks' you will need in building.

While still on the subject of creating a vision for your company, it is important to note that many people confuse the notion of being self employed with being a Business owner. There is a clear difference between these two words and many people do not recognise the difference. The job of a Business owner is to create a Business which works with or without his or her intervention. Just like the job of the owner of a Football club is to run the club, buy the best player, employ the best manager and ensure that the team performs to the best of their abilities and score goals. You will not see the owner of the football club going on to the pitch to play except if he decides to.

The reason why I gave the example above is simply because one of your aim as a Business owner must be to create a Business that has a systematic way of operating so your Business can still generate income whether it has your input or not at any given time. Even if you are starting off as a 'one man band', it is essential to have a long term aim of creating a self dependant Business. The main difference between a Business owner and a self employed individual is that a self employed individual is one who has basically created a job for himself or herself. This is a person who runs a one man Business which totally depends on him and has to work day and night to keep the Business alive.

Here is a typical example, you can find a mechanic who owns a shop and he is the one who is the main point of contact for all the customers, he is the main mechanic in the shop and he is the one who is known and trusted by the customers. As the owner of the Business, if he falls sick or is unable to work for a long period of time, it means that the Business cannot operate as he is the main focus of the Business and he has made himself the main trusted mechanic for all the customers.

The alternative would be a Business owner who owns a mechanic shop, employs some mechanics to work for him, employs a manager to run the shop and oversees the whole operation. With this type of model, this Business owner can afford to take days off work and still ensure that the Business will run effectively or even choose to open another branch of his shop without disrupting the service of the existing shop.

This is just an example of the difference between a self employed person and a Business owner. Your aim should always be to become a Business owner and have your Business working for you and even if you starting off on your own, this should always be your long term aim. This gives you a chance for expansion and also ensures that you have a sustainable Business that can last even when you are not around. This also gives you a better chance of selling your Business for a better value.

Back on the issue of creating goals or vision for your Business. When you are thinking of starting your Business, you should ask yourself three questions:

- What do I want to achieve in this Business over the next 6 months?
- What do I want to achieve in this Business over the next one year?

• Where do I see this Business in the next five years?

With these three questions, you are able to set your short term and long terms goals. Your goals should be SMART, i.e. Specific, Measurable, Achievable, Realistic and Time-bound.

Example of goals can be:

• In the next 6 months, I would like to have 10 clients on board
• In the next one year, I would like to have opened a second branch
• In five years time, my company would have 100 staff members and 10 branches

These goals are specific, measurable, achievable and time bound. You need to determine what you want to achieve, when to achieve them, how you would achieve them and what resources you would need to achieve these goals.

There are several reasons why it is important for you to create long and short term goals for your new Business; here are just some of the reasons:

Focus: When you are very clear about your long and short term goals or vision for your Business. It gives you a clear focus in terms of how to run your Business and which areas you should be putting your energy into. When we talk about your focus, there are several opportunities that may arise for your Business but your long and short term vision will help you determine which one to choose. Setting daily tasks in your Business will also be made easier once you have set goals.

For example, there could be opportunities to expand your Business in a different country but you could decide to turn down the opportunity as you want to focus your attention on one country. Your long term goal could be to develop a known and trusted brand in your country within the next five years, so it would not be appropriate to go into another country within that time frame. It is therefore important to understand your long term vision

Direction: This is probably one of the most obvious reasons for having a long term goal or vision. You cannot know the direction to take in your Business if you do not have a goal or vision for your Business. This goes back to the analogy of the bus journey; you must first understand your destination before choosing the bus to take. As well as choosing the right bus, it is also important to understand the route which you will take on your journey. This can also be known once you have determined and decided the destination.

This will not only affect you as the Business owner, but your staff or employees which you take on in the future or even at the start of the Business. If they do not have a clear direction, they will be clueless as to what to do and how to work in your Business as they will not have a guide or goal to work towards. Your job as the Business owner is to create a clear vision which your whole company will run towards and will give directions to both you as the Business owner and your partners or colleague. This will also help ensure that no one goes off the path and you are able to check that everyone is on the right path.

Patience: One of the attributes that are needed in running a Business is patience. Most businesses do not make a profit within the first 1-5 years and it is important for you to develop an attitude of patience during the foundation-building stage of your Business.

It is however important that you are patient as a Business owner when building your new Business. A long term vision or goal means that you are working towards a destination and your current position is not where you aim to be in the next 5 years. This ties very well with your financial forecast and this is one of the reasons for having a good financial forecast. You must ensure that you know the breakeven point of your Business, so that you understand when you will make back the initial money which you have invested in your Business.

Knowing the destination of your Business will always give you the confidence needed to keep going even when you are not bringing in as much as you hope to do at any point in your Business. The analogy of the bus ride can also be used to further describe this factor. If you are going on an 8 hour bus journey, you will be aware that this is a long journey and you will be prepared for it in terms of food provisions, finances to buy snacks during the break and any other things that you may need during the journey.

While you are on the journey, you will sit patiently on the bus during the ride and you will not have any reason to complain until you complete the full 8 hours when you expect the bus to have reached its destination. Even then, you will still be patient, knowing that there may have been traffic delays or any other cause for delay which has caused the bus to run over time. The point is that you will have no choice but to be patient through the bus ride as you know where you are going and you have a rough idea of how long it will take you to get to the destination, therefore any discomfort which you may face during the journey will be accommodated till you reach your destination.

In order to develop patience through the rough times of your Business, you must know where you are going and the rough time it will take you to hit your goal in terms of finances and other aspects.

Performance Measurement: Having a long term goal in your Business also means that you can measure your performance and those of your employees and partners. When you have short and long term goals, you can measure the success of your company based on these goals. Not only the success of the company as a whole, but the performance of your employees also be measured.

For example, you may want to have a company that turns over 1.2 million pounds in the next five years. Your short term goals could be for your staff to take on a new client every week which will add to the revenue which is being realised weekly. By having the long term financial goal, you are able to know how many clients you will need weekly which is a short term goal and you are able to measure the performance of your staff to check if they have met this target or not by looking at the amount of clients which they have signed up every week.

Money Management: This is also one of the important reasons for having a long term goal or vision for your Business. As a new Business owner, you may be the one monitoring your finances until you are either able to afford an in-house accountant or hire an independent accountant to manage your accounts. You may be in charge of managing the spending of your money and you must therefore ensure that you are wise with the spending of the income and revenue that comes into the Business.

Having a long term vision means that you are able to manage your finances based on the long term aim of the Business. For example, if you have the aim of rapidly expanding your new Business in the next 3 years, you will aim to put some money aside that you will contribute towards the expansion and this will reflect in the spending of the company finances. The ways which you treat your finances will always reveal your long term aspirations for your company. Some Business owners have a short term mindset where they spend every income which comes into the Business without looking to save some towards future projects or upcoming plans. Falling into this trap means that you will keep borrowing and running your company into debts as it grows.

Time Management: Apart from your finances, one of the most important asset which you have as a Business owner is your time and you have the choice of how you spend it. When you are just starting off as a new Business owner, you will find that you are able to determine your own time management and your goals will help determine your day to day time management. The tasks you take on and the priorities for each task will depend on your goals.

When creating your long and short term goals, there are several areas that you may want to consider. Here are some of them:

a) Size: When you are looking at the long and short term goals of your Business, you must know how big you would want your business to become in near and long term future. There are various companies out there that started off as a 'one man band' and are now multi billion pound large Businesses. You need to determine whether you want your Business to stay as a small Business or your aim is to expand it to a medium or large Business.

b) Revenue: This is one of the most important goals which you will need to set for your new Business. When you start your new Business, you must have some sales forecast and also draw out some of your other financial statements to predict where your company will be financially in the near future. Your forecast will include how much income should be coming into your company as these figures will help you to know important facts such as your breakeven point and the financial health and sustenance of your company in the long run.

c) Location: Another factor that you may want to consider when setting your long term goals or vision is where you will be based as a Business. You may decide to start your Business in one location with the aim of moving to a different location in the future. For example, you may choose to start your Business in a certain part of your city due to the cost of hiring a premise whereas your main target customers are located in the main city centre which is more expensive. Your long term aim will be to change your location at some point and you will be working towards this.

You could also decide to move your Business overseas in the future and trade in another country and you will take this into consideration at the start of your Business.

d) Area of Coverage: It is important to know the coverage for your products or services in the long term future. Your coverage refers to how far you would like to products or services to go in order to serve clients. For example, your products or services could be available to customers internationally, nationally, or locally and you must know your area of coverage in the long term. Even if you start off serving your local community you may have the intention of expanding in the future to other parts of your country. For example, you may start off running a coffee shop in your local area with the aim of opening up other coffee shops in other areas of your country and you will have this at the back of your mind as you are starting the Business in order to ensure that you know when to open the next shop and also put some money aside which will assist you in the expansion.

e) Number of Staff: This is linked to the size of your Business but it may also be important to know how many staff will be employed by your company in the long term. This will also be determined by certain factors that have already been discussed before such as your plans for expansion and the area of coverage. For example, the more areas you choose to cover with your products or services, the more likely you are to employ more staff.

Knowing the number of staff which your company will employ in the long term means that you are able to use this when producing your statement of finances. For example, this will reflect in your expenses and expenditure forecasts.

f) Number of Clients / Customers: Your aim must always be to gain more clients in your Business. Customers are the lifeblood of any Business as they bring in the income of the Business. You must be able to make a prediction of how many clients you would like to have in your Business in the next 6 months, 1 year and 5-10 years.

As previously discussed, even if you only have a handful of clients at the start of your Business, it is important to project the amount of clients or customers which you would like to have in your Business in the long term as this will help you to set targets on how many customers to add to your client list in a given period. Knowing your number of clients means that you are able to determine if there is a need for expansion. For example, if you find that there is a sudden demand for your products or services and you are planning to have a significant increase in your customer base, compared to that which you have now, then you may need to expand and open up more premises in order to accommodate the expected demand or increase.

These are just some of the areas which you can use when drawing up your long and short term vision or plans for your company. You may find other areas which can be used for your Business and you can always add that to the list.

ACTION POINTS

After learning the importance of setting long and short term goals for your Business, it is time to apply this to your idea. Using the factors stated above, clearly state out your short term and long term goals for your company. Your goals should include:

• Six Month Goals

• One Year Goals

• 5 year Goals

• At the end of the task, calculate how much you need to spend to get the resources needed to set up your new Business.

Under each time frame, clearly set out your SMART goals.

STEP 5

DIFFERENTIATE YOUR PRODUCTS/ SERVICES

"Competitive strategy is about being different. It means deliberately choosing to perform activities differently or to perform different activities than rivals to deliver a unique mix of value."

MICHAEL PORTER

It has been mentioned more than once in this book already that differentiating yourself or setting yourself apart from competitors is Key to success in your new Business. This chapter helps you to understand how to do this. As a new Business, one of the problems you may encounter is competition from existing Businesses in your chosen industry. When talking about differentiation, ask yourself a simple question:

"What makes my products / services different from my competitors?"

Developing a differentiation method for your new Business is essential for gaining competitive edge in your new industry. This is even more so if you are going into a saturated market. Differentiation refers to the process of distinguishing your products or services from your competitors. You must be able to stand out and capture a good share of your market in order to survive as a new Business.

One of the fears which new Business owners have when it comes to the issue of differentiation is that they will end up losing some customers in the process. The best way to look at this is to flip it the other way round. Stating your niche in your market means that your customers trust that you can give them the best service as you are dedicated to them and you are an expert in that area.

Let's take a look at the shaving stick example; certain shaving sticks are specially targeted at women which means that the stick will be tailored to a woman's needs and the target market can be assured that this stick will give the best result such as less irritation and a smooth shave on their body.

Throwing yourself out there as a 'jack of all trades' could mean that you are not tailored to any specific type of customer and you are not known to be an expert in any area.

Importance of Differentiation

- Firstly, differentiation is very important to the success of your Business. It will help your customers remember your Business when they need your products or services. Your aim is to ensure that you are the first company that comes into your customer's minds when they require your products or services. For example, when you think about the fast food industry, the first name that probably comes to mind is McDonalds.
- Differentiating your Business will ensure that you can compete with existing

Businesses in your industry or market. When starting off as a new Business, you are probably going into an industry where competitors are already established. The questions that you've got to ask yourself is this:

"Why should customers choose me over existing companies?"

Your customers will be asking themselves the same questions before choosing to buy from you.

- Differentiation can help with creating the branding for your company. Differentiating yourself means that you are able to create a unique brand to fit in with your differentiation method. E.g. creating a product targeted at children means that you can brand it to appeal to a particular age group.

- Differentiation helps you create a niche for yourself which sets you apart from competitors. Once you do this, you will be seen as an expert in your niche area. For example, if you provide personal development coaching for women, you will be seen as the 'go to' person for personal development related problems with regards to women and your advice will be sought on this issue. This will easily attract your targeted customers.

- Differentiation can give you an advantage in setting your prices. For example, if you have a product that has a strong differentiation method and it attracts a good market share from the start, you may have the flexibility of increasing your price above the market average. An example of this is a dry cleaners that does home pick-up and delivery, this means that it stands out from its competitors who may not offer the same extra service and hence play about with prices.

Differentiating your Business also refers to defining your Unique Selling Point (USP). Unique selling Point is particularly important when it comes to selling yourself or your Business as well as marketing and promoting your products or services. You must be able to state the uniqueness of your products or services especially when you are competing in a crowded industry.

As a start-up, there are different ways of finding a unique selling point. Firstly, you must understand what your competitors offer. You must research the same products or services offered by other companies and look at features that may be missing. Another way to set yourself apart is to look at what your potential customers want and see if existing products are offering them already.

There are several methods which you can use when thinking about differentiating your Business. Here are some of them:

Target Market
One of the ways of setting your Business apart and differentiating yourself from competitors is by picking a segment of the market and focusing your products on that part of the market.

With this method, you are targeting a niche which means that your products or services will be directed at that segment of the market. This will help you stand out and attract those types of customers more effectively.

E.g.,regarding the shaving stick example again, the colour of the shaving sticks which are targeted at women is pink which means that women are able to easily identify with this colour.

In order to chose this method of differentiation, all you need to do is look at the market which you are about to enter and examine which demographics are not being targeted and this can give you an idea of where to position yourself.

In the next couple of chapters, you will be able to learn how to define your target customers.

Special Skills
There are special skills which can be used to form a USP. For example, you could be a fashion designer who makes handmade clothing. This special skill can be used to differentiate between yourself and other fashion designers.

Handmade clothing are known to be of a high quality and expensive. Defining yourself as a designer of handmade clothing means that you automatically stand out from the clothing market in general and customers will tend to think about you when they want quality materials.

Look at a special natural ability which you have developed which can set the way you deliver your products or services apart. Also look at skills which you have gained from experience which can add extra value to your customer experience and this can be used to stand out from the crowd. Ask yourself this question:

"What unique skill do I have that can make my Business stand out from competitors?"

Another example could be a website designer who focuses on developing Flash websites, he could decide to go further and focus mainly on 3D Flash websites which gives him a USP in the market which other competitors might not have.

Added Value

In earlier chapters, I mentioned that one of the ways of finding a new idea is by looking at existing products or services and looking for missing features.One of the ways to differentiate yourself from your competitors is to add an extra value and 'go the extra mile'. 'Going the extra mile' means that you look at products or services which exist and look at ways which you can make them better. This will also help you stand out as your customers will be attracted to the extra benefit which you offer.

For example, you could open a dry-cleaning service in your area but decide to offer home delivery and pick up which means that this will give you a competitive advantage as customers would not have to travel to get their clothes dry-cleaned.

When you advertise or promote yourself, this will be your USP. You will highlight this in your marketing materials in order to grab the attention of your customers. Look at the product or service which you are about to introduce to the market and ask yourself:

"What extra value can I add to this product or service to make it stand out?"

Location

One of the ways to stand out and differentiate oneself is also to offer an existing product in a different location.

Your location and your area of coverage can set you apart from other market competitors and ensure that you are targeted at a particular area.

For example, you could open up an Estates Agents in a particular area and serve the local area. This may give you a competitive edge over other national Estates Agents as this means that you are very familiar with the area.
The subject of choosing your Business location and how to use it as a USP will be covered in the next chapter.

Experience

This has already been mentioned in previous chapters but it is worth mentioning again. One of the most effective ways of differentiating yourself in your market is the level of experience which you have gained in the industry.
When you look at certain industries which are highly saturated such as the Estates

Agency market, you will see that certain agencies will highlight their years of experience in their marketing in order to attract new customers.

Your level of experience in your industry is usually seen as a 'trust factor' by your customers. Customers will usually trust you to deliver a quality service once they know that you have been in your industry for many years. For example, when you're looking for a Mechanic to fix your expensive Mercedes, you will look for a mechanic with years of experience in fixing a Mercedes. The reason why you would probably do this is because you want to be sure that your car is in the hands of someone who knows what they are doing and someone who has handled similar cars over a long time.

As a start up, you may say that you haven't had any experience in running your Business and therefore this method wouldn't count for you. When you haven't had an experience of running your own Business in that particular industry, the next step will be to look at the previous experience which you may have gained in the same industry while working for another company.

For example, you may want to start up a PR company and you have worked for a top PR company in the past with clients such as NIKE, McDonalds etc. You can use the fact that you have worked with these big brands in your previous jobs as a USP in your Business. This means that your customers can be assured that you have experience in delivering PR services to top companies, therefore your level of delivery will be high.

ACTION POINTS

Looking at all the differentiation methods given above, what are your own differentiation methods?

1. Write methods which you are using to differentiate yourself from competitors.

2. Once you have chosen your differentiation methods, write down a statement highlighting your Unique Selling Point as a Business. Ask yourself this question:

"What makes me different from my competitors?"

STEP 6

CHOOSE YOUR BUSINESS LOCATION

"Sometimes when you innovate, you make mistakes. It is best to admit them quickly and get on with improving your other innovations."

STEVE JOBS

Choosing Your Business Location

Location of your Business Premises

Geographical coverage of Products / Servicess

The subject of choosing your Business location is not one to be taken lightly. As previously mentioned, one of the ways to differentiate your Business is through the location of your premises and the coverage of your products and services. Your location can be used as a differentiation factor when dealing with customers or defining your Unique Selling Point (USP). Below is an example of a conversation between new Estate Agents in an area and a potential customer.

Estate Agents: Good morning madam, we've seen that you have put up your property for sale and we would like to put this property on the market for you.

Customer: I'm sorry but I already have other major Estate Agents trying to sell it on my behalf and it hasn't been a huge success. What makes you think you can do a better job than these other Estate Agents?

Estate Agents: Our Estate Agents are based locally therefore we have a very in-depth knowledge of the local area so we are able to market your property to our database of local clients waiting for a new property in this area.

This is just an example of a scenario where a Business location can be used at an advantage over competitors especially in a populated market. Due to the Estate agents focusing on a particular local area, he is able to use his expertise in that local area as a differentiation method from other general estate agents.

Defining your location is not limited just to your local area, you can use a country as a niche location e.g. a bank with customers in the UK which also has its call centres in UK will have a competitive advantage over another bank with a call centre in an overseas country as this means that customers are able to get in touch with the customer service department easier and the service offered will be relatively more efficient.

From these examples, we can see that it is essential you state the location of your Business when defining or describing your company. It is quite important to let the customer know where you are based and where the distribution of your products and services cover.

When looking at the location of a business, there are two factors that have to be considered. One is the location of the Business premises and the other is the area covered by the distribution of the products and services supplied by the Business.

Business Premises location:

The location of your Business premises can either give your new Business an advantage or act as a disadvantage. When starting a new Business, you can either decide to work from home (depending on the type of Business you are starting) or you can acquire an office from the offset. Whichever route you choose to take for your new Business, you must understand that not only can your location act as a differentiation method, but you are likely to 'plant' your business in that same location for a very long time. Therefore careful consideration has to be taken when choosing a Business premises. The type of location chosen as a Business premises will depend on several factors such as available finance, size of Business etc. You will find out more about this subject in the coming chapters.

Many people argue about the importance of carefully choosing the right location for a Business premises. Let's explore some of the factors that affect your choice of premises location:

Type of Business: Your type of Business will determine the location of your Business premises. E.g. an online company may only require an office space which will accommodate its staff or use for meeting with customers while an online retail company may require a large warehouse for storing all its goods and an extra office space to accommodate its staff.

For shops and other retail businesses, location is a key factor for them as it is important that they are located in an area that will attract their target customers. If your Business relies on passing trade such as a convenience store, you would want to be located in an area where your target customers can see you.

For example, aconvenience store or newsagent will be located in an area close to Public transport. Other types of Businesses can be operated from home, for example, an accountant can decide to operate from home and meet his clients in their own offices and that way he can save a lot of cost on office space.

Cost/Budget: The location of your Business premises will also depend on your budget allocated to this cost. The location of a Business can influence the cost of the premises. Apart from rent costs, there are other costs that can vary depending on the location, such as Business rates etc.
Therefore, in order to choose suitable premises for your Business, the cost involved has to be weighed against the amount allocated in your budget. Generally, premises located in the city centre tend to be valued higher than those that are located outside city centres. This is another major factor that can affect your choice of Business location.

Convenience: This is one of the most important factors to consider when choosing the location of your Business premises. Your premises must be located in an area which is convenient for your customers to visit.

For example, an accountancy practice with clients located all over the city of London would need to make sure that their Business premises is located in a central area which is easily accessible for all customers.

This factor will apply mainly to Businesses which rely on constant face-face interactions with customers. Apart from customers, it is also important for the Business premises to be located in an area which is convenient for employees. The location should be easy for employees to travel to. Depending on the number of employees involved in the day to day running of the business, factors such as good public transport links or parking facilities will make it easier for employees who do not live in the local area to travel to work.

For some types of Businesses which require constant interaction and dealing with suppliers such as convenience stores or retail shops, it is important to consider the distance to the suppliers when choosing a Business premises. If you a planning to own a Business which may require you to make regular visits to the suppliers, then you will have to take this into consideration when choosing the base for your Business.

Number of Competitors: Before choosing to operate in a certain location, it is very important to carry out an in depth research into the area i.e. the type of market in the area, the number of competitors already located in the same area and the approximate number of potential clients for your Business in the same area.

One of the most important facts to know is the number of direct competitors in your chosen location. This is crucial because you may not want to be too near your competitors, depending on the type of Business. For example, several Estate agents can compete in the same local area as long as there is enough demand from customers in the area.

<u>Geographical Coverage of Products and Services</u>

This has been briefly mentioned in the first Step 2 of this book. Your Business premises can be different from the area that is covered by your goods and services. This subject ties in with your method of distribution. The coverage of your products or services refers to the areas where your products or services will be available for customers.

Your areas of operation can be different from the location of your Business premises. For example, your office can be based in Sweden while your customer base is located in United Kingdom.

When describing your Business to customers or potential clients, it is important to state which areas are covered by your products or services. Clearly defining your areas of operation means that you are able to attract the right clients and you're able to identify your right market.

For example, a car dealership that is based at and operates in New York has to specify this on their website in order to attract customers who may live in the local area that require their services. There will be no point in a customer in Sweden contacting this dealership to purchase a car from them except if the car is an exclusive model which is only available in that area.

When differentiating your Business, you can use your areas of operation as a Unique selling Point e.g. Two car dealerships operating in two separate countries will not be in direct competition with one another as they will have different markets in their countries. This can be used as their differentiation factor.

When considering your Business idea, you must clearly identify and define which areas would be served by your products and services. There are certain types of Businesses that are likely to cover a wider geographical area than others. For example, online companies tend to be able to reach a wider audience than companies that have physical trading places such as convenience stores and supermarkets.
The internet has become a very influential tool in helping Businesses reach a wider audience and many companies are making use of this tool but there are still certain businesses that can only serve particular areas due to the nature of their activities. E.g. A Dry Cleaning Company may only be able to serve its local area due to logistical and cost-saving reasons.

Your marketing strategies and advertising methodswill determine how wide your target audience will be; therefore you need to take your method of distribution into consideration. There is no point advertising or making your products or services to customers in several countries if you are only able to access local customers.
With Businesses that operate from physical premises, they tend to have several premises in different locations in order to cater for local customers in the area. Examples of this method can be found with coffee shops such as Starbucks, fast food restaurants such as McDonalds, supermarkets such as Tesco, etc. Most of these types of Businesses cannot trade online therefore physical Business premises

are essential.

There is no limit to the size of your target market or the areas which you intend to distribute your products and services to as long as you are able to justify this through your distribution methods and marketing strategies which will be used.

Another factor which needs to be considered when choosing the areas of operation would be the cost involved in distribution. For example, an online clothing boutique whose premises is based in the United Kingdom can choose to distribute its products to customers in Africa as long as it considers the cost of delivering the goods to Africa and this cost does not make the product too dear. There would be no point in offering a service or product to customers in a particular area where the cost of delivering the products will be more expensive than the products itself. It is therefore important to be sure of the method of distribution for your products or services before deciding on which areas to cover with your products and services.

It is possible to have different distribution methods for different areas being targeted for your Business. For example, if you plan to trade in different countries but have your main base in one country, you may decide to use resellers to distribute your products or services in other countries or offer franchises in these countries.

Other factors to consider before making the decision about areas of operation are the resources available to you for distribution of your products or services. For example, a take-away restaurant in one town can decide to serve several other towns as long as it has the mode of transport which can be used to deliver the food being ordered by customers or else it will be impossible to deliver on the marketing promises.

There areseveral digital Software and devices which have been made available to make it easier to reach your target market such as Skype and other software. For example, a Business coach based in London can decide to open up his services to clients as far as Australia by conducting the coaching sessions through Skype. Other types of Businesses with this type of digital advantage include web designers who can take on projects without having face to face meetings with clients as long as they can assure the client of their quality of work.

It is very important to take all these factors and much more into consideration before deciding on which locations to target as failure to deliver on marketing promises will result in bad representation of your Business which will in turn ruin your company's reputation.

ACTION POINTS

From the points mentioned above, it is obvious that the issue of choosing a location for your Business premises and area of coverage for your products and services is not one to be taken lightly.

1. Write down the areas which you have chosen to locate your Business Premises

2. Make a list of the areas where your products or services will cover.

STEP 7

DEFINE YOUR CUSTOMERS

"The golden rule for every business man is this: Put yourself in your customer's place."

ORISON SWETT MARDEN

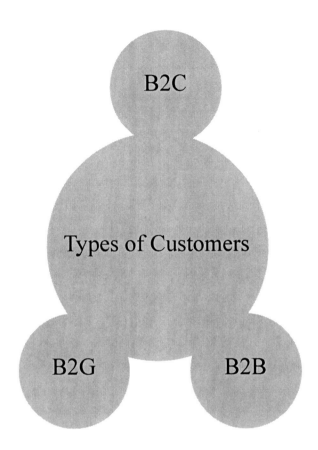

As a start-up, one of the first principles you must understand is that your customers are the lifeblood of your Business. The success of your Business depends on your ability to please and retain your customers. When you are starting a Business, one of the first issues that you must address right from the beginning is the definition of your target market. It is very important to be sure of whom your products or services are aimed at. Your target market is simply those who are likely to buy your products or services. They are the people you take into consideration when developing your products or services.

Still dealing with the subject of differentiation, I have already mentioned that one of the methods of differentiation is by targeting a specific segment of the market. Your branding, marketing strategy, promotion and price will reflect your target market. Defining your target market is very essential as it gives you a clear and specific direction when setting up your Business.

One of the easiest temptations that a Business owner can fall into when setting up a new Business is the urge to "please everyone". You must resist the temptation to be too general when developing your marketing strategy. One of the biggest mistakes you can make as a new Business owner is to think that by appealing to everyone in your market, you can get a larger slice of the market share. That is like aiming one bullet at two birds at the same time; there is a high chance of missing both birds. A company who tries to become all things to every customer is heading for failure as it will end up attracting the minimum number of customers.

The issue of targeting a specific audience can be explained using an easy to understand scenario. If someone is diagnosed with a rare heart disease which can kill him within a couple of months if left untreated, such a person has two choices to make: He can decide to visit a general doctor who 'might' have a solution to the problem or he might decide to visit a cardiologist who is a heart specialist and has a higher probability of providing a cure for the disease. With such a life threatening situation as this, it is important for the patient to be assured that whoever he deals with can give the right answer to his heart problem within the required time frame.

Some might argue that surely, you cannot compare this scenario to that of a costumer and a Business. It is however important to note that just as the person with the heart disease will want to use a specialist and competent doctor, a customer will rather buy products or services from a supplier who is an expert in their market and targets the segment of the market where he or she falls into. This applies particularly to Businesses that supply services e.g. a black woman in need of hair styling would rather search for an afro-Caribbean hair stylist rather than looking for a general hair stylist. This is because she knows that visiting this particular stylist means that she is guaranteed to be styled by a person who knows about her hair texture, knows the right products to use for her particular type of hair and is familiar with the hair styles used by afro-Caribbean women.

This is just one example and it can apply to several types of products and services. Customers would want to be sure that they are receiving the best products or services and the best way to guarantee this is to make sure that the supplier's products or services are tailored towards them.

Every successful company has a target market in mind for their products or services. It is possible for one company to target multiple markets or target different customers with different segments of their company. This is common among large corporations and Businesses, for example, Gillette has different types of shaving sticks directed at different types of audiences. They have shaving sticks for men and those for women. The two shaving sticks are produced by the same company but the marketing, promotion and advertising are different as they are aimed at different target markets.

Huge profitable companies such as Amazon probably started off with a focus on a specific target market and they built a strong customer base within this market before expanding.In the case of Amazon, they started off just selling books for a couple of years before expanding into selling other products such as DVDs, CDs and other product.

One of the problems which new Business owners face is the willingness to turn down business opportunities when it doesn't fall into their target market. It can be difficult as a new Business owner to keep your focus on a specific segment of the market and establish yourself as an expert in that market. This can prove to be a long process as you need to introduce yourself into the market and gain acceptance from the customers. This therefore forces some new Business owners to abandon their focus and fall into the temptation of pleasing everyone and appealing to every segment of the market.

Let's take a scenario where you walk into a room wearing a yellow jumper when everyone else is wearing a black jumper, you will definitely get noticed and get picked out of everyone else. You must pick out a segment of the market which you want to appeal towards and use this as a differentiation tool.e.

Targeting a specific segment of the market means that you are not afraid to leave out the remaining segments of the market in your marketing strategies, promotions and advertising. Once you identify your target market, your advertising, marketing promotion, branding etc. must reflect your chosen market. This is very important as your target market must be able to embrace your company as a whole through every medium which you use to project it. Your aim is to be seen as the expert by your target market and they must embrace your brand as a whole.

One of the simplest ways of identifying your segment of the market is to look at the whole market and consider which areas of the market is being ignored or hasn't been populated by other businesses. For example, if you want to set up a web design company, you could decide to focus on university students starting new Businesses and offering affordable pricing to this target market. This means that you have to take the age group and affordability of the market into consideration when planning your strategies. So with this example, all you are doing is entering an existing market but focusing on a particular segment of the market.

Becoming an Expert in Your Target Market

As stated earlier, one of the easiest ways to differentiate your Business and establish yourself among your target market is by becoming an expert in your field or your Business industry and the market which you are targeting. To become an expert simply means that you are seen as the 'go to' person about your products or services and your target market. An expert is someone who has valuable resources and can offer advice and tips to customers regarding their products or services. For instance, to be known as an expert in an accounting practice means that you are able to offer your clients tips and advice on how to keep up with their accounts in their Businesses.

For example, a company like Research In Motion which produces the blackberry smartphones originally designed it for Business Professionals but as time went on, they started targeting younger audiences by designing stylish smart phones with different colours, affordable prices, multicoloured casing, introduction of the app world where users can download several applications and games and the vast popularity of its Blackberry messenger. Through its use of the Blackberry messenger application, it has established itself as an expert in the Smartphone market for young adults.

One of the advantages of establishing yourself as an expert in your field is that you are able to set your own standards such as pricing. Customers will be willing to pay almost any price for your products once you are seen as an expert. One of the easiest ways which people are seen as experts in their field is by offering free advice or information through avenues such as blogging, article writing, company website etc. For example, an accountant who targets start-up Businesses can decide to write regular blogs showing its customers how to keep their accounting up to date and save money in different areas of their Business. This will give the accountant exposure and attract the target market to his blogs, hence seeing him as an expert in the accounting practise targeting their market.

It is important to note that there is no point in being an expert in your field if you are unable to project your knowledge to your target market. By sharing your knowledge with your desired target market, you will become quickly known as an expert and this can in turn lead to sales, contract offers or other opportunities. You must find ways of communicating your knowledge and expertise to your target market as this will draw them to you and will ease the stress of marketing and advertising.

There are several methods which you can use in establishing yourself as an expert in your industry to your target market. Here are some examples:

Social Media: In this age where social media has created a new buzz among the existing and upcoming generations, it is important that you tap into the opportunities that have arisen with the emergence of the social media age. There are several platforms which can be used to reach your target audience. There are social media platforms for Businesses, individuals, interest groups etc. Social media platforms such as 'Twitter' are places where you can easily make your expertise known to your target audience. It is a place where you can interact with your target market and offer free advice and tips.

Through social media sites such as 'Facebook', 'Twitter' and 'LinkedIn', you are able to interact with your target market, create a fan base that both trust you and look to you for expert advice and information. By creating this fan base, you are building confidence in people who know your expertise and are able to recommend you to others who may need your services.

Here are some of the top social media sites that are recommended for Businesses to join in order to relate to their target markets:

• Facebook
• Twitter
• LinkedIn
• Youtube

New social media platforms are being developed and it is important for you to keep a look out for those which can benefit your Business.

Blogs: Blogs are one of the most effective ways of projecting your knowledge to your target market. A blog is fantastic if you have a lot of information that you want to share with your target market on a regular basis. With a blog, you can share what you know, offer advice, give people opportunities to leave feedback, give your opinion about events and current affairs that relate to your profession. A good blog will always encourage readers to keep coming back for more, keep them engaged, interested and informed.

Blogs can either form a part of your website or you can use several websites that provide free templates for creating blogs such as:

- BlogSpot
- Tumblr
- WordPress

With these sites, you can create free blogs and share them through your social media platforms to your target market. An example of a blog for a wedding planner could be a weekly diary of the weddings she's planning where she shares the ups and downs of planning weddings and shares tips on how to plan a successful wedding. You can apply the same method to your Business, where you can share weekly or regular tips on how your target market can make the best use of your products.

Free Online Webinars: With the introduction of several software and platforms that enable online seminars to take place without physical contact, webinars are becoming increasingly popular. With webinars, you can host free sessions where people who may be interested in your products or services sign on and listen to your tips or advice on your area of expertise.

For example, a Business coach could host free webinars teaching Business owners how to grow their Businesses or offering steps on how to get more customers, your aim is to teach on an area of your profession where you want your clients to see you as an expert. Webinars are becoming popular among Business owners in bringing their target market together without accumulating more costs.

Videos: Earlier on, I mentioned 'YouTube' as an essential social media platform for new Business owners to make themselves known as an expert. YouTube creates a platform for uploading free videos and this is becoming very popular for different experts in their industries. Creating a video is a way to show your target market the wealth of knowledge which you possess by uploading several videos such as "how-to" videos which teaches the audience easy ways to carry out several tasks in relation to your profession.

For example, a company that supplies hair styling products could create regular videos on how to effectively use their hair products and show the audience which products to use, how to use them, how often etc. Creating videos can build trust quicker than any other platform as your audience are able to put a face to your company and people tend to trust you quicker when they are able to see your face. Here are the most popular video platforms where you can start uploading free videos

• YouTube

• Vimeo

Speaking Engagements: For some types of professions, speaking engagements are one of the easiest ways to be seen as an expert. For example, if you are a social media consultant, you may decide to host regular seminars giving your target market tips on how to use social media for their Businesses, hence projecting your expertise to your target market.

Speaking engagements allow you to relate with your target market as a group under one roof. You can either decide to hold your own speaking engagements or you can decide to look for regular slots in other events. Your aim would be to deliver speeches relating to your profession and prove your knowledge to your target market.

Becoming an Author: At this very moment, you are reading a book which is giving you tips and advice on how to start your own Business. This is one of the ways of projecting your knowledge and becoming an expert in your field. Becoming an author is one of the most effective ways of reaching your target audience on a much wider scale. Becoming an author doesn't only apply to writing books but it can also mean that you write short articles which you can send out to your target market on a regular basis. Articles can either involve tips or advice which you give to your target markets regularly regarding products or services which you offer. Articles can either be sent out via emails or through social media platforms or in newspapers and magazines.

The second type of authorship which you can use is books. Books will give you the opportunity to reach your target audience across several geographical locations where you cannot physically reach. A decision to write a book will depend on the location which your Business is involved in and how wide you are planning to cover in terms of your audience. The books written must cover topics or areas where you aim to be seen as an expert. Books can also be used in conjunction with speaking engagements as you can sell your books at the engagements in order to earn some extra money.

These are just some of the ways in which you can project your expertise to your target market, hence drawing them to your services. Other ways include visiting regular networking events where your target market will be present, using media coverage such as TV, Radio etc.

Types of Market

When talking about choosing your target market, there are different types of markets that you can sell your products or services to. These are Governmental organisations, Businesses and Individual Consumers. When describing these three types of market, they can be categorised using the following terminologies:

• B2G (Business to Government)

• B2B (Business to Business)

• B2C (Business to Consumers)

Before you can look at targeting a specific segment of a market in order to use it as a niche, it is important to understand which type of market your Business falls under from the list stated above. Choosing the type of market which you will focus on depends on several key factors such as:

⇨ Your type of Business
⇨ The requirements for your products and services in the market
⇨ The area of operation for your Business and the prominent type of markets in the area.
⇨ Your distribution channel. This is discussed further in upcoming sections.

It is possible to get involved in more than one type of market, but you must state which segments of each market will be targeted and what products or services will be targeted at each market. For example, an events planning company can choose to offer corporate events and weddings where corporate events can be offered to Businesses such as Team building events and wedding events can be offered to individual consumers and this will both fall under B2C.

Let's look at these different types of market and examine the differences between each one:

B2G – Business to Government: This is the process of marketing and selling your goods or services to Governmental organisations. It's quite simple, you are the Business and you are trading with organisations which are government owned. This type of marketing applies to Businesses which aim to supply their products or services to public sector organisations, local governments, state government or federal government.

B2G provides avenues where Businesses or organisations are able to bid for Government contracts on different types of projects and opportunities. Contracts can include cleaning contracts for local councils where cleaning companies can bid for this or they can include different types of programmes which the Government wants to introduce and needs companies that can carry these programmes out.

Many types of Businesses can decide to offer their products or services to the Government ranging from a website designer to a Security company. You would need to look at the segment of the Government which you would like to serve, e.g. you could decide to supply office supplies to the local councils offices and this means that you will target every local council office in different areas. This means that you can establish yourself as an expert in that market where you will be attracting all the local council offices when they need office supplies.

With B2G, you will have to look out for contracts which are put out by the Government using several platforms such as local council websites where prices are already set for each contract and you will have an opportunity to bid for the contract where you will provide the service or supply the products enlisted in the contract.

B2B – Business To Business: B2B is the process of selling and marketing your products to other Businesses or companies. This is where one Business sells its products or services to other Businesses and they in turn either resell it, use it to produce the products which they already offer or use it in support of their operations.

A simple and common example of a B2B process is a broadband company that supplies telephone line and broadband services to Businesses, a web designer that supplies websites to Businesses, a stationary company that supplies office supplies to Business owners etc. These examples are Business to Business marketing where the customers are using the products or services for supporting the operation of their company. Another example is where a company sells its products or services to other companies and they are able to resell them to consumers. An example of this is a manufacturer of skincare products which decides to sell its products at wholesale prices to retail stores who in turn resell them to consumers.

The third way which your company can get involved in B2B marketing is by supplying products or services which can be used as a component in producing their products. An example of this could be a company that produces its own range of body care products but need the components which will be combined to make each product such as the oil needed which is part of a component to make a body cream.

You have to determine whether you are able to offer your products to other Businesses. This can be determined by the type of products which you supply. A simple Business idea such as a mobile food delivery service can be classified under the B2B marketing where a food company decides to supply lunchtime menu to local Businesses and their staff. Another example is where a gym offers corporate membership to Businesses where their staff can visit the gym on the company membership.

B2C – Business to Consumers: This is the process of selling your goods or services to individual consumers. This is one of the most common types of marketing. This is where you sell your products or services straight to consumers for personal use. When choosing this type of marketing, you must understand that your method of distribution will be direct.

Examples of Business to Consumer marketing are coffee shops which supplies its coffees for personal consumption, a hair stylist who offers hair styling services to customers, a wedding planner who plans wedding for individuals etc.

You must determine whether you want to sell directly to customers or you want to go through other Businesses as resellers and you must also determine whether your product is suitable for individual consumption or it is aimed at Businesses. For example, if your company is selling office furniture, your customer base would be primarily Businesses as these are the type of market that would need office furniture but you might have some individuals who want to purchase office furniture for general use at home.

<u>Stating Your Demographics</u>

Whichever type of markets you chose to operate in it is important, as previously stated, to focus on a particular segment and this is how you can create a niche for yourself and you can use this to differentiate yourself from other competitors in your market.

Demographics are the attributes or characteristics which can be used to describe a particular population such as age, gender, ethnicity etc. This is what you can use to separate a segment of the marketplace from the remaining section of the market. For example, if you choose to market your products or services to individual consumers, you may choose to focus on young adults aged between 12-24 and this means that you have used the age demographics to focus your marketing on a particular segment of the whole market. You can even go further by using the age and gender demographics as the factors for differentiating your Business. For example, if you decide to start a life coaching Business, you can choose to focus on women under the age of 35 years. With this segregation, you have chosen to use both the age and gender demographics in developing a niche.

The same method can be applied to the B2B markets where you can choose to differentiate yourself from your competitors using the different demographics such as type of Business, location of the Business, number of employees, size of Business etc. These can be used to differentiate the type of Business which you supply your products or services to. For example, an IT support company can differentiate itself by focusing on small Businesses with 1-20 employees. With this type of differentiation, the supplier is able to target a specific segment of the Business market by using the Business size and number of employees.

The same principle applies to Governmental organisations. There are certain attributes that will differentiate the various types of organisations e.g. level of Government such as local Government, central Government etc.

Your aim is to look at your type of market, examine the attributes which you can use to differentiate the market and look at which demographics you will be focusing on.

ACTION POINTS

Defining your customer is Key as you have learnt from the main text. In order to clearly define your own target market, answer the following questions:

- Which type of market (s) will your product or services be selling to?
- In each market, what demographics are you focusing on?

The next step is to list down your products or services and write the type of market that each product or service will be serving next to it.

.

STEP 8

FIND YOUR CUSTOMERS

"Customers will want to talk to you if they believe you can solve their problems."

JEFFREY GITOMER

Once you have clearly defined your target customers, the next thing is to actually go out and look for these customers to buy your products. The main issue to consider is where exactly you are going to find your target market and how you are going to reach them. Every type of Business has certain strategies that work best for them and your aim should be to get the best Return on Investment (ROI) you put towards your marketing and promotion. As previously mentioned, without customers you cannot build a Business. You must ensure that you spend enough time looking for new customers. At the start-up stage of your Business, you can risk doing everything else but looking for new customers.

When I mention return on investment, you may automatically start thinking about money but this is not the only form of investment that can be made in marketing. There are some form of marketing that may not cost you money but can still cost you time and time is an investment that cannot be regained once lost. Therefore, your aim should be to know the best form of marketing that works best for your new Business and know the ones that generate the least amount of leads and sales.

The reason why it is important to first clearly define your target market before finding them is because you must know what you want before you start looking for it. You cannot spot an opportunity for Business if you are not sure of what you are looking for. Finding your target customers doesn't only refer to the strategy you will use, but it also refers to the way you will use each strategy and how much it will cost for each strategy chosen. You will understand this a bit more as we go along in this chapter.

Marketing Strategies

As I have mentioned several times already, one of the basic fundamental principles of a Business is that you must acquire customers as they are the ones that bring in revenue for your Business. Therefore it is important to know where you are going to get your customers from. This is known as marketing strategies. This means that you are able to create a plan which will enable you to effectively reach your target market. As mentioned earlier, every Business has different avenues or strategies that will work best for them. For example, a Web designer may pay more attention to online strategies in order to find his clients as many Businesses, both large and small, now have a strong online presence through social media and own websites.

A wedding planner might also find that social media could be the best place to find clients as it makes it easier to promote and interact with the target market on a wider scale. For a Business to continue to survive and become successful, it must always find new avenues to use in reaching its customers and know which one works better than others.

Marketing isn't just about creating awareness of your products and services, it is also about retaining your customers, creating loyalty and making sure that your products and services are constantly in the mind of your target market. Your aim should be that your company would be the first one that comes into people's mind when they are in need of your products or services.

The first step to take in order to achieve this aim of creating customer loyalty is to look at the means of finding your customers. This is very essential as it will help you with effective advertising and promotion and ensures that your products and services are placed in the right places. With the emergence of several types of technology over the years, the strategies that can be used by Business owners to communicate with their target market are fast becoming limitless.

Generally speaking, the marketing strategies used in promoting your products and services and gaining new customers can be categorized into four groups:

- **Offline Marketing**
- **Online marketing**
- **Word-of-Mouth marketing**
- **Joint Ventures**

Offline Marketing

Offline marketing is one of the oldest and most traditional forms of marketing. This type of marketing is one that most people are familiar with as they always seem to produce results and can easily be achieved without the need for any technological expertise. Offline marketing basically refers to those marketing strategies that do not involve the internet. Despite the domination of the internet in this age, many businesses still turn to the traditional style of marketing as it still delivers good results.

Here are some examples of offline marketing:

- Print – Such as Magazines, Newspapers, Fliers, Yellow pages etc..
- Television
- Radio
- Billboards
- Posters
- Seminars
- Conferences

Offline marketing can either be cheap or expensive and this depends on the size of your business and your budget which is allocated towards marketing. For example, an IT consultant with three members of staff would probably not chose to use the billboard for their marketing campaign. Remember that your marketing campaign must be able to deliver a good Return on Investment (ROI) which means that it must deliver a good profit margin on the money spent.

With the emergence of the internet where most individuals and businesses are found online, one would think that this will cause a demise in the offline marketing strategies but this is not so. Many large organisations still choose to opt for the offline marketing campaigns over online marketing campaigns such as TV advertisement.

Online Marketing

As mentioned earlier, the emergence of the internet has caused a revolution in marketing and this has made it easier for Businesses to reach their target market. The internet has made it easier for Businesses to reach their target market in any part of the world without having to spend off-the-chart prices. Online marketing is basically making use of the different resources available through the internet in order to reach your target market. Online marketing, in most cases, offers Businesses the opportunity to reach a vast number of people at a fraction of the price that it would cost for using an offline marketing strategy.

For example, if you wanted to distribute and market your skin care products in 6 countries, it would cost large sums of money to do this through the offline strategies such as TV broadcasting and billboards in the different countries but using the internet means that you can use such mediums as social media in order to reach the wide market intended.

With online marketing, you can define your target market and tailor the marketing towards the right audience using different techniques. There are several types of strategies that can be used online, some of them are:

• Ad placements: This is where you place an advertisement for your company on different websites and you pay for each time the advert is viewed or clicked on. This means that you must ensure that your advertisement is effective and it is placed in the right places.

• Email marketing: This is also becoming popular among several companies where databases are collected or acquired from different sources and regular emails are sent out to the contacts on the database in the form of press releases or regular newsletters. You must make sure that your database of contacts consists of your target market which means that there is a high chance of getting sales from the email marketing campaign sent out. Email marketing can be used to announce new products, promotions, special events etc. You must however be very careful not to fall into the trap of misusing the email marketing tools by sending out SPAM emails.

• Social Media: This type of marketing has quickly gained momentum with the emergence of social networking sites such as Facebook, Twitter, LinkedIn, Myspace etc. These social network platforms have become really powerful tools in the online marketing world that they have attracted the attention of politicians, musicians, celebrities and many other important figures as well as major firms all over the world. This type of marketing gives you the opportunity to reach a wide variety of individuals and Businesses without having to spend so much. With these social networks, there are various ways of utilising them to achieve full potential for your Business e.g. Businesses are able to create fan pages on Facebook and also use paid advertisements where they can define the market to whom the adverts will be shown.

• Affiliate Marketing– Affiliate marketing has also grown over the last few years and it is gaining popularity in the online marketing world. This is where you allow other website owners to promote their products or services on your website in return for a commission or you promote your products or services on other websites in return for commission on every sale or lead generated. With affiliate marketing, it is quite affordable to set up and maintain. It is however important to be sure that the website where you aim to place your products or services are targeting the same audience you require.

As time goes on and the internet continues to evolve, new forms of online marketing strategies will definitely arise. There are other strategies which have not been mentioned above such as Digital marketing, Search Engine optimisation, Video Marketing, Banner Marketing etc.

Word of Mouth Marketing

Word of mouth marketing is probably the most powerful form of marketing that exists. This is based on the 'trust' factor where people buy products from you because they have developed some form of relationship with you. It is said that people buy from people they know and trust and this is why word of mouth marketing is very effective. As a business owner, you should never underestimate the power of word of mouth marketing as this can either build up a company or destroy it.

For example, Facebook currently has nearly one billion active users and the list is growing every day. This number was mainly achieved through word of mouth advertising. You must make sure that you create 'raving fans'. These are customers that are so satisfied with your products or services that they immediately recommend it to friends and family.

Word of mouth marketing can take place in several ways. One of the most common types of word of mouth marketing which has emerged in the Business world is Multi-level Marketing (MLM) which is where a person or employee sells and refers products or services to others with the intention of them buying the products and also becoming a promoter of the product. With this system of marketing, there is an incentive for promoting the products to others as the salesperson receives a commission on his or her own sales and a smaller commission on the sales from each person he or she convinces to become a salesperson. This type of marketing is also known as network marketing, referral marketing etc. There are several companies that have taken up this type of marketing with which they have built a wealth of poeple actively promoting their products and recruiting other promoters and earning commission for each sales made.

There are other word of mouth marketing that can be used such as attending networking events to promote your goods and services to potential clients. There are other ways where word of mouth can come into play e.g. if someone recommends your products or services in a blog or article, this will also give your product some credibility as long as the person is a well respected individual in his or her profession.

Joint Ventures

Joint ventures, when done the right way, can be the most effective and easiest form of marketing. Joint ventures occurs where you look for Businesses that share the same type of customer with you and you partner with the company to promote your product to their customers in return for either a fee or other form of agreed incentive.

For example, as a Business start-up coach, I constantly work with accountants and web designers and the reason for this is that we both share the same types of customers. An accountant is bound to get customers who are starting off new Businesses who are in need of my services and the same applies to web designers as new Businesses tend to need websites.

Therefore the next step to take would be to have an arrangement whereby the accountant may promote me in her newsletter to her clients and I give her a commission for every client I receive through her newsletter or we can develop a joint venture partnership where we both promote our services to each other's clients: I promote her accountancy services to my clients and she does the same thing hers.

Another way to develop a joint venture is to host a seminar where we can both invite our customers and the content of the seminar will cover accounting tips and also give some Business advice, hence promoting both our Businesses.

The next question that you need to ask yourself is this:

"Which Businesses share the same customers as me?"

Once you make a list of some of these companies, you can start approaching them to see the different ways that you can work together, even if it means that you drop your fliers in their office. Always remember that both parties have to benefit in a joint venture. You offer your customers and they do the same.

There are some factors that will determine the type of strategies which you adopt, some of these are:

- The type of Business you have: Different types of Businesses will use different means of advertising. For example, a convenience store owner will use different types of promotion and advertising from an online boutique. You must understand your customers in order to know where to find them.

- The area covered by your products and services: Another factor to consider when looking at places where you can find your target market is the areas covered by your products and services, e.g. an international Business with the intention of distributing its products and services in multiple countries will be better off utilizing online strategies for its Business where it will be able to contact its target market without having to invest so much in advertising and marketing.
If you are a local Business, then your marketing strategies will be more offline and word of mouth focused and even joint venture with local Businesses will work very well.

- The resources available: This is a very important factor to consider. After stating all the possible ways to find your customers, you will be restricted by the resources which are available at your disposal. For example, there is no point in choosing online marketing strategies to reach your target market if you haven't got the resources to do so or use door to door promotion when you don't have the printed materials and other resources needed to do so.

Before choosing the avenue to use for reaching your customers, it is important to look at the resources you have in place and which ones you need in order to do so. This will give you an idea of the avenues which you can pursue for gaining new clients.

• <u>Your Type Of Market:</u> By now, you should have a definite idea of which market you are planning to enter. This will help determine your avenues to getting new customers. The strategies used for finding Business customers will be different from those used for consumers. For example, there will be no point in a local convenience store using 'LinkedIn' to find its customers as this is a social media platform suitable for Business group customers.

• <u>The demographics of our Target Market:</u> The demographics of your market will help you tonarrow down the right avenues to use for finding your customers. This is why it is essential to narrow down your target market to a clearly defined form where you can use the criteria given when listing down the avenues employed in finding your customers. Some businesses spend unnecessary funds on advertisement which does not bring in the required revenue because they use the wrong avenue.

For example, if you choose to advertise through a newspaper, you must know the newspaper that appeals to your target market and use this or else you will not be able to get a good return on your investment. An IT company which offers software services to Businesses will probably choose to advertise in a Computer magazine at it knows that the target market will probably be interested in this type of media. It is therefore important to have clearly stated your target market before thinking about which avenue to use for getting your clients.

These are just some of the factors that you need to consider when making a list of strategies which you can use for gaining your customers. Remember that each Business is different and your niche market will determine where you find your customers.

Avenues for Each Strategy

After defining the strategies that can be used for finding your target market, it is important to break this down further into the avenues that can be used for each strategy. This will be tailored to each Business idea. Remember what we said in the previous section, each Business will have a strategy which works best for them; therefore it is up to you to know what type of strategy works best for your Business. When we talk about avenues which will be used for each type of strategy, it means that you need to know how to utilize the strategy chosen. For example, if you chose to use Social media marketing, it is not enough just to know this but you must identify which social media platforms to use and how you are going to use each one effectively.

For example, a web designer may chose to use social media as part of his marketing strategy. The next thing that he has to think about is the types of social networking sites and platforms which will be useful to his type of Business. He may decide to use Facebook, Twitter, LinkedIn and Youtube as avenues for the social media marketing strategies. What he needs to think about is how he will be utilizing each avenue. Below are examples of how this can be done:

Facebook: Create a Group page
          Create a Fan page
          Create a paid advert
          Create a 'friends' page

Twitter: Create a twitter account

LinkedIn: Create LinkedIn account
          Join different Business groups to promote services

YouTube: Create YouTube Account
          Upload several free 'how to' videos to promote services

This is an example of how to break down the different avenues that can be used for a particular Marketing strategy. The same format can be used for any type of strategy chosen for your Business. For example, if you choose to market your products at several networking events, you will need to apply the same principle, break down the different names of events that you plan to visit and list down how you are going to use each event, how often you will be visiting and having an understanding of how each event can impact your Business.

Knowing the different avenues that can be used with your chosen strategy means that you are able to clearly define your budget, know the resources which are needed and clearly measure your return on investment for each strategy you have chosen to use.

<u>Resources needed and cost of Marketing</u>

While still on the subject of finding your target market, it is also important to consider the resources needed in order to apply the strategies. Resources refer to those items or things that will aid you in implementing the marketing strategies which you have chosen to use for your Business. For example, if you chose to market your Business through TV advertisement, one of the main resources which you will need is the advertisement video which will be played by the channel. When looking at the use of word of mouth marketing such as networking events, some of the resources which will be needed are Business cards, Fliers and other promotional materials.

It is important for you to clearly define what resources are needed for your marketing as this will help you to know the budget and costing which will be allocated to this part of your Business on a periodic basis. Once you choose the resources you need, you will be able to find ways by which you can acquire these resources.

The cost of your marketing is determined by the type of marketing strategies which you have chosen to use and the resources needed. It will also depend on factors such as:

- Your Type of Business: Different types of Businesses will depend on certain types of marketing more than others. For example, Businesses which use multilevel marketing will spend less money than those who depend on online or offline marketing as multilevel marketing tends to be cheaper to implement and there are less overhead costs.

- Size of Business: The size of a Business will usually influence the amount which the Business dedicates towards its marketing. For example, the amount of money spent on marketing by IBM will definitely not be the same as a new IT consultancy. You have to 'cut your coat according to your size'. This means that you are aware of your capability financially before allocating a budget to your marketing and committing to spending a certain amount of money on the resources.

- Amount of Resources needed: As stated earlier, the total cost of your marketing will depend on the amount of resources needed. If you mainly implement strategies which do not require lot of resources, this will help keep your total cost low. There are some form of marketing which do not require a large amount of money such as Social media marketing where it requires time, effort and expertise rather than physical resources.

• Type of Strategies implemented:As stated earlier, the type of marketing which you chose to use will determine your budget. There are some types of marketing that require a high budget while some require a low budget. For example, there are some offline marketing strategies that cannot be afforded by many small Business start-ups such as Billboard or TV advertising and hence why many small Business start-ups tend to go down other routes of marketing.

ACTION POINTS

1. Write down the type(s) of marketing strategies which you will be using in your Business.

2. Under each strategy, write down the specific methods which you will use e.g. Offline marketing - fliers distribution

3. Under each strategies listed down, define how you will use each one.

4. Make a list of the resources which are needed to apply to your chosen strategies.

5. Once you have written down your resources, calculate the total cost of your marketing at the start-up stage.

STEP 9

CHOOSE YOUR BUSINESS PREMISES

"Give the public everything you can give them, keep the place as clean as you can keep it, keep it friendly."

WALT DISNEY

Once you have defined your customers and thought about how you will find them, the next step to take into consideration is your Business premises. This is another factor that many people do not carefully consider before going into a new Business. Many take it for granted and realise along the way that it has an effect on their new Business.

Your Business premises refer to where the activities of your Business will take place. There are several types of Business premises that can be used by a new Business and there are several factors which should be considered when choosing your type of Premises. Here are some of them:

- Size and layout of the premises: There are certain types of Businesses that require a particular type of layout for the premises, e.g. your Business might require two or more separate floors or same floor with separate sections which can separate different departments.

- The structure and appearance: Both the internal and external appearance and structure of your premises may need to be considered especially if you are in certain types of industries such as the fashion industry where you will be interacting with your clients at your premises.

- Special facilities: You may require some special facilities at your premises. The facilities could be needed for staff or customers e.g. reception area, toilets, kitchen and parking spaces– for deliveries or customers, including disabled customers. These would depend on the size of your Business.

- Planning Permissions: You may need to acquire some planning permissions to create your suitable premises. Examples of buildings which may require planning permissions are those used for Businesses such as Nursing homes, Nursery etc

- Structural Requirements:There are some special structural requirements that may be taken into consideration when choosing your Business premises e.g. some art galleries might require high ceilings for their premises.

- Long Term Expansion: You may have a long term plan to expand your Business in the future and therefore you may want to consider acquiring a premises that will give the flexibility for expansion.

- Size of Business/ Employees: The size of your Business at the start can also affect the type of premises needed e.g. a one-man Business might be started from Home while a Business that has up to 10 employees at the start might need an office space to accommodate its staff and equipments.

Type Of Business Premises

As stated above, there are different types of Business premises that can be acquired when starting your Business. When thinking about your Business idea, it is important to know the appropriate type of premises for your Business as this will reflect on the cost incurred and affect your projection of figures.

As a new Business, you have to set a start up budget allocated to different resources required for your Business. The budget allocated towards your Business premises will depend on the finance options available to you and the importance of a Business premises to your Business at the start-up phase. The budget placed on a Business premises will determine what type of premises can be acquired.

When making a choice for your Business Premises, it is important to be aware of certain costs that can be incurred in the process. These costs can depend on the method of acquisition (i.e. whether the property is being bought or rented). Here are some examples of costs that can be incurred when obtaining your Business premises:

• Purchasing Cost: This can apply when buying the property.

• Legal fees such as solicitor's fees: this can apply both for rented and bought properties.

• Professional fees e.g. surveyors fees

• Fittings, Fixtures, alterations and decorations: This will depend on the requirements of the premises.

• Ongoing regular Payments: These are payments which are made towards the premises regularly e.g. rent, mortgage, service and utility charges, including water, electricity and gas.

• Insurance:Building and Content Insurance and any other types of insurance that is needed.

• Other Rates: There may be other rates that need to be paid, depending on the country and the requirements of the Governments for Business owners. E.g. Business Rates.

There are various types of premises that you can choose for your new Business, here are some examples:

Commercial Office space: An office space can be simply defined as a physical space that is used for office operations such as creating working areas for staff, meeting clients, day to day managing of your Business. There are three main types of office spaces which are home-office, commercial office and serviced offices.

Commercial office spaces are those which most people are familiar with as they are the ones which are used by majority of Businesses e.g. accountants, solicitors, online Businesses etc. These types of office spaces are very popular and exist in different places in stand-alone buildings, converted warehouses and several other forms. They can be leased, rented or purchased.

Commercial offices spaces are available in different sizes, depending on the number of desk space needed and employees involved in the company. There are even cheaper options where Businesses share the same office space in order to save costs.

In order to consider choosing a Commercial office space for your Business, you will need to consider some of the factors which have already been mentioned and the suitability of this type of premises for your Business.

Serviced office space: Thisis another type of office space that is becoming popular with several Businesses due to the convenience. This type of office space is very similar to Commercial offices. They are also known as 'Managed Offices'. A serviced office space is a commercial office space which comes with many services and furnishing. These may include furniture, equipment, telephone lines and infrastructure which are already in place for the Business to use.

The services and furnishings available with each serviced or managed offices vary from property to property, however, nearly all serviced office spaces include basic furniture and utilities in the price of the rent or lease. With serviced offices, they usually include security of the office building. There are other add-ons that can be acquired with serviced offices such as business machines, conference room and other services depending on the property.

Businesses may decide to choose serviced offices due to the simplicity of it and it is easier to move in and out of a serviced office as most equipment are readily available, unlike commercial office space. You can also decide to choose a serviced office space over a commercial office space if you do not need the office space for a long period of time. There are some Businesses which require office spaces for a short period and therefore a serviced office will be perfect for such Businesses.

Home Office Space: As a new Business Start-Up, working from home may prove to be a better option for you at the beginning rather than buying or renting the premises. Of course, it is important to take other factors into consideration before choosing to operate from a home-office. A home-office may be appropriate to a Business owner who spends majority of their time working in clients' offices e.g. an IT Consultant or PC repair.

Working from a home-office may not be appropriate if you intend on having regular face-face meetings with clients. It may not be appropriate to run a Business from home if it attracts a high number of visitors to the property. Rented properties may also create legal problems in terms of using them for home offices as this could conflict with the terms stated in the tenancy agreement.

A home-office doesn't necessarily have to be a dedicated room. It can be a section of an existing living room or family room or a converted space in the house. The type of space used in the house will depend on your requirements and the equipments that need to be fitted in the space.

Virtual Office: Virtual offices are becoming more popular with Business Start-ups as it allows a small company to look bigger than it is. Virtual offices can be cost effective especially for Businesses that trade in several locations without the need for setting up offices in these locations. They are available in several countries and they are perfect for Businesses who are constantly involved in travelling.

A virtual office refers to offices which are not owned by a Business but allows the Business to make use of some of its services such as mailbox, registration address, rental of office spaces and rooms and receptionist services. With a virtual office, several Businesses can make use of the services available in one building and office spaces and meeting rooms can be used on a "pay as you go" basis. Several virtual offices offer different levels of services and it depends on the needs of your Business. E.g. you may only require a professional registered office and mailbox or a receptionist service.

This type of office space is becoming more popular with Business start-ups especially those who are working from home. A virtual office may also be ideal for a Business which requires a lot of travelling around or meeting clients across different locations. You can use this to portray a level of professionalism to your client.

Retail shop: A shop refers to a building or a part of a building where goods or services are sold or exchanged. There are several types of shops and they can be located inside large shopping malls, high streets or residential streets. A shop is a place where customers go to purchase goods or services.

A shop can either sell physical goods or deliver services in the building. Examples of shops where physical goods are sold are supermarkets, convenience stores or general stores. Example of shops that deliver services to its customers are nail shops, barbershop, hairdressers etc.

You may need a shop for trading if your business requires selling products or delivering services to customers regularly on face-face level. There are exemptions for companies with online stores, this means that the Business can either adopt a home office or a commercial office space while trading online and sending out the products to the customers through the post.

Your requirements will determine whether your Business needs a retail shop or not.

Public Houses (Pubs): Public houses (also known as pubs) are drinking establishments. They are different from bars or cafes. They are establishments where there is sale and consumption of varieties of alcoholic and non alcoholic drinks. Pubs tend to focus more on wine and beers while bars tend to serve cocktails and mixed drinks.

Apart from providing a place to consume and buy drinks, pubs also act as place of entertainment and often act as a focal point for local areas such as villages and towns. It usually acts as the main meeting points for local people in a particular area. The owners of public houses are usually referred to as pub landlords.

Running a public house is a specialist type of Business and these types of premises have special requirements such as laws and regulations due to the consumption of alcohol.

Warehouse: A warehouse is a commercial building where goods are stored. Warehouses are usually located in industrial areas in cities and towns. The structure of a warehouse usually contains loading docks where goods are loaded and unloaded from trucks. Warehouses are usually used as Business premises by Businesses such as manufacturers, importers/exporters, wholesalers, those in the transport business etc.

There are some companies that can hugely benefit from having a warehouse or storage facility. For example, big online companies that are involved with the sales of products usually keep their good in large warehouses which can then be shipped to customers. Large companies such as 'Amazon.com' own several warehouses where different products are stored and shipped out at the request of customers.

Apart from warehouses being used to store goods and products by large companies, there are now stores and supermarkets that can also be called warehouses as they are structured like them but are open to trading for the public. An example of such stores is 'Costco'.

Factories: A factory is a building, usually industrial, which contains heavy equipments and machineries for processing or producing specific goods. It is a place where labourers either manufacture goods manually or supervise the machines that are manufacturing the goods.

Factories are usually based in large warehouses but the set-up and facilities involved are different from that of a normal warehouse. Factories are usually used by Businesses in the Manufacturing industry where they manufacture goods from scratch and send them out to other companies who either sell them on as wholesale or distribute them to retailers.

Using a factory as a Business premises is probably one of the most expensive Business premises that one can chose to obtain as a premises for starting a new Business.

Restaurants: A restaurant is a building where food and drinks are prepared and served to customers in return for money. Apart from serving and preparing the food, they are also generally consumed in the same premises while some restaurants offer a 'take-away service' where food can be purchased on the premises but taken outside to be consumed.

The structure and outlook of restaurants vary in size and design. This is at the discretion of the owner and the type of restaurant which it is. The outlook of a restaurant is generally determined by the type of food being served in it.

The type of premises needed for a restaurant depends on your requirements and the style and design of the restaurant.

There are also other premises which can be considered for your Business such as hotels, nursing homes or care centres, nurseries etc.When making the decision, examine the factors which have already been stated and look at the requirements of your new Business.

Methods of Acquiring Your Business Premises

As stated earlier, an important factor to consider when choosing a Business location is the cost involved in acquiring the Business premises. This is important as you must be able to cover the cost of the premises from your start-up budget. Of course, this will not apply if you decide to start operating from home to save start-up cost.

Some Businesses can decide to purchase their premises while others can decide to rent. E.g. a nursing home can decide to buy a piece of land to build its new site on while an I.T Consultancy company can decide to rent an office space with monthly rent payments in order to accommodate its staff and use as a Business premises.

Choosing the method of acquiring your Business premises is a decision which has to be carefully considered especially since your premises will probably turn out to be your largest fixed asset. It is important to examine the pros and cons of both buying and renting the Business premises as this gives you an opportunity to decide on which one suits your type of Business. For example, your business could require constant change of location; therefore it would not be suitable for you to purchase the premises.

Here are some of the pros and cons of both renting and buying a property.

Renting a Property

Many businesses decide to go through the rental route as it gives more flexibility with moving location, depending on the length of the contract

The advantages of renting depends on the terms of the agreement with the property owners e.g. length of the contract, terms and conditions of tenancy etc. When you rent a property, you agree to occupy the property for a period of time as agreed in the tenancy agreement and pay the agreed rent on a periodic basis. Depending on the terms of the contract between you and the Landlord, there can be allowance for the rent cost to be reviewed during the rental period. When renting a property, there are certain costs that may be incurred such as refundable deposit, legal fees and other professional fees.

One of the major disadvantages with renting a property is the difficulty which may arise if you want to move out of the property before the end of the contract period. Another disadvantage of renting a property is the fact that the terms of the contract may contain some restrictions to the use of the premises which may affect the smooth running of your Business.

If you choose to go through the rental route, then it is important to check the terms stated in the contractual agreement very carefully before agreeing to take the property. You must also be fully aware of the length of tenancy agreement as stated in the contract and make sure that this falls in line with your future plans and projection for your company.

Buying a Property

Depending on your budget, you can decide to purchase your Business premises rather than rent it. When purchasing your premises, depending on the country and the type of Business, you may decide to buy an existing building or buy a piece of land to build on. When you are buying a property, you have a choice of buying it in two separate ways, through a freehold or a leasehold.

When you buy a property on freehold, it simply means that you own the property outright. It means that you have the freedom to do as you wish on the land as long as you are able to obtain the planning permission and this is subject to the law of the country. E.g. you can decide to paint the building or change the style or design of the building as long as it is allowed by law and the planning permission.

This type of purchase is beneficial where your Business requires a custom design or a change in the existing structural outlook of the premises. With freeholds, you have the ability to set your own terms of use for the building.

The second means of purchasing a Business premises is through leasehold and this is similar to renting the property. When you're buying a lease, you are essentially buying nothing more than the right to occupy a portion or the whole building for a given length of time. There is a one-off lease ownership payment which covers you until you either sell the lease or it runs out. In addition to the one off payment, there are also regular payments to be made known as ground rent and maintenance.

Leasehold purchase generally occur where the premises is in a building that comprises of more than one unit such as a block of offices in a building and other commercial property. With a leasehold property, there are restrictions to the alterations that can be made to the property and this depends on the terms stated in the lease.

If you choose to go through the purchasing route, it is important to make sure that you are aware of which type of property you are purchasing.

Here are some of the advantages and disadvantages of buying a property compared to renting.

Advantages:

o There is no threat of rent increase once you purchase the property.

o When you purchase the property, there is a chance that it will increase in value which means that your business benefits from capital gains.

o You have more freedom on what to do with the property such as sub-letting it in order to generate extra income.

o With a purchased property you have a lot more flexibility with the design of the premises which means that you can design the premises to suit your business needs or even rebuild or expand if need be.

Disadvantages:

o When purchasing a property, there will generally be a demand for a deposit which can vary between 20%-30% of the value of the property in advance. This may be hard for new businesses to raise

o With purchased properties, you will have to finance any breakage and upkeep of the property which will in turn incur more cost.

o If the value of the property drops, it will have an impact on your business capital.

o When you purchase a property, it is possible for the rate for your mortgage to increase which will in turn increase your monthly payments. This can be bad for your business especially where there is not much revenue coming in.

o Once you purchase the property, there is less flexibility to adapt to change in circumstances e.g. if you need less space or you need to move to a different location.

Whichever route you choose to take for acquiring your new premises, you must make careful considerations before making the choice.

ACTION POINTS

After looking at the different types of Premises and getting an understanding of each type of premises, answer the following questions:

• What factors do you have to consider when choosing your premises?

• Which type of premises will you choose for your Business?

• What avenue will you choose for your premises? i.e. renting or buying.

• What are the costs which will be incurred with your choice of premises?

STEP 10

EXPLORE YOUR COMPETITORS

"The competitor to be feared is one who never bothers about you at all but goes on making his own business better all the time."

HENRY FORD

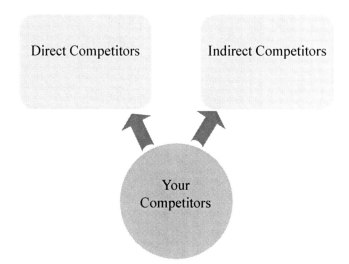

In step 5, I broke down the notion of differentiation. I mentioned that differentiation meant to be able to stand out in a populated market or having a USP (Unique selling Point) which is able to set your company apart from the rest of your competitors in the sight of your potential customers.

When looking at differentiation or establishing a niche, you cannot effectively do this without being aware of the competition in your market place. You must know the Businesses that operate in your marketplace and your industrywhich targets same or similar audiences as you.

A competitor is simply a company or Business which is in the same industry or similar industry as you which offers the same or similar product or service to yours. A well known example of competition is McDonalds and Burger King or Pepsi and Coke. Competition can either be good or bad both for you as a Business owner and also for your customers. Let's look at some of these:

• For customers, an industry with lots of competition means that there is a variety of choices when it comes to pricing and this means that there will be a good chance of getting the products or services at a competitive price. Competition in the market place gives the customer a big advantage as it means that they can get the products for the best price. When new products and services are introduced into the market place, the company usually has the power to start out with a high price, but after a while, other companies begin to make similar products which cancompete with it and this causes a drop in price as competition increases. Once this happens, customers are then given a choice of products to choose from with competitive prices.

- Having a large number of competitors in a market or industry also means that companies in that particular market or industry have to constantly innovate in order to gain a larger market share. An example of this can be found in the fast food market where companies such as KFC, McDonalds, Burger King, Pizza Hut are competing with each other. Even though these companies may not be in direct competition, they are in the same industry and therefore they constantly innovate by inventing new products into their range and offering different types of deals in order to stay ahead of their competitors. It is very important for a Business trading in a competitive market to continually innovate and find new ways of staying ahead and attracting new customers.

- A market with various competitors means that the products or services being offered are available to consumers with different choices to make. In a competitive market, once competition grows, products of poor quality or ones which are overpriced are usually pushed out of the market by the consumers due to availability of choices.

- One of the biggest disadvantages of having a high level of competition in your market is that the profit margins may not be high as it means that the demand for your products or services will be spread across several suppliers. It is very important for you to consider this when focusing on a target market because it may affect your profit margin. This basically means that the more people are supplying your products or services to your target market, the less money is likely to come into your pocket as it means that your customers have a choice to make when choosing suppliers.

Looking at some of these impacts which competition has on your Business, it is important for you to ensure that you develop your differentiation method in order to gain as much market share as you can and therefore increase the sales and profit that comes into your Business. This will also give you an advantage when setting your prices as it means that you have the freedom of setting your own prices especially if you aim to bring in a new product into a new market.

For example, when Apple invented the IPAD, they were able to offer their own prices without fear of competition as there were no similar products directly competing with them at the time. As time has gone on, however, other Tablet PCs have arrived in the market which means that there will be competitive pricing and use of other innovative avenues in staying on top of the market.

One of the reasons why it is important for you to explore your competition before jumping into a new Business is the issue of intellectual Property and Patenting which deals with protecting your Business concept against any emerging competition. This applies especially where you choose to invent a new product or service which may not previously exist. If you however aim to deliver a product or service which already exists in the market or similar to an existing one, it is important to consider the Businesses that are both in direct or indirect competition with you.

The importance of being aware of your competition cannot be stressed enough, there are certain factors that are affected by the competition in your market, and some of these are:

- Your pricing: The way you price your products or services must reflect the current trend among your competitors, therefore it is important to know what your competitors are offering in terms of pricing before setting your own as a new Company in the market.

- Your Niche: Without being aware of the competition and what they supply, it is impossible to differentiate yourself and define your niche. You cannot differentiate yourself from someone when you are not aware of their method of operation. This is why it is important for you to have full understanding of the competition in your market.

- Your Advertisements and Promotion: This is a very important part of your Business. It is important to understand the strategies which are currently being used in your market by your competitors so that you can know which ones work and which ones don't. Knowing the strategies currently in use which do not work means that you will avoid going through the same route and wasting time and effort.

- Your Branding: This is another aspect of your Business that could be affected by your competition. When you're entering a market, it is important to know the trend which is being used in terms of branding by your competition. When we refer to branding, we are talking about the company name, logo, colour scheme and all other things which projects the image of the company to its customers. You must know how your competitors brand themselves to the market as this will help with your research and aid in forming your corporate identity.

When thinking about your competitors, there are certain questions that come to mind, here are some of them:

• Who are your competitors?

• What products and services do they supply?

• What are their Business objectives?

• What are their strengths and weaknesses?

• What strategies do they currently use and how successful are the strategies?

• What threats do they pose to your new business?

• What are their prices for the products/services supplied?

• Are they in direct or indirect competition with you?

As previously mentioned, you will encounter two types of competition in your new Business; these are direct and indirect competition. Now let's examine the difference between these two:

Direct Competitors

Direct competitors are those who offer the exact same products or services that you offer to the same target market. As stated earlier, a target market is simply a segment of a whole market which you have chosen to sell your products or services to. For example, you could choose to sell your products to young adults aged 30 years old and under. This means that you have picked out these demographics from the overall market and chosen to sell your products or services to them.

A direct competitor is simply another Business that sells similar products to yours or the same products and you both target the same segment of the market. To be a direct competitor simply means that another Business is competing directly opposite you for customers. For example two 'Chicken and Chips' fast food restaurant on the same road would be in direct competition with one another. Burger king and McDonalds would be in direct competition with one another.

You need to be aware of your direct competitors as this will help with structuring your strategies such as pricing, marketing, advertising etc. For example, an estate agents opening in a new area has to be aware of other estate agents in the same area which offer the same services so it can know how to differentiate itself from the others and the strategy that will be used in entering that particular market in the location.

You cannot identify your direct competitors if you haven't clearly defined your target market and established where you stand in your market. The easiest way to find out information about your direct competitors is simply to visit their premises, use their services or test their products. Your job is to find weak areas and look for weaknesses in your competitors and use this to your own advantage.

Whatever your Business is, it is very important to know who is directly competing with you. It is however possible not to have a direct competitor as you may be inventing an innovative product that doesn't exist in the market at the moment. If you decide to enter a monopolised market where you have protected your product or service with Copyright, then it is possible to run a Business with no direct competition but this is quite dangerous as it means that there is a tendency to become complacent.

Indirect Competitors

Indirect competitors are those Businesses that offer products or services which are similar to yours but do not have the exact same target market as you. These are Businesses that offer products or services that can be bought by your customers in place of yours. Products or services offered by indirect competitors can offer the same benefit and results as yours even though it is not the same product.

In order to find out who your indirect competitors are, you can ask yourself the following questions:

• What is the end benefit of using your product or service?

• What other products or services offer the same end benefit?

After answering these questions, then you can find your indirect competitors. When discussing the issue of direct competition above, the example of the two 'chicken and chips' fast food restaurant was given as being in direct competition with one another as long as they trade in the same location, an example of an indirect competitorcould be two chicken and chips shops in two separate locations or a chicken and chips shop and a pizza take away restaurant in the same area.

In the first example, two 'chicken and chips' shops in different areas are in indirect competition because, even though they offer the same products, they have different types of customers as these types of shops tend to focus on the local areas and customers in the local vicinity. The pizza take-away shop and 'chicken and chips' shop in the same areaare in indirect competition with one another because they might supply different products to the same client base, but their products cannot be used in the place of the other.

For example, when you are hungry, you can either choose between a pizza or chicken and chips fast food restaurant. These two businesses may be in the same industry, but they supply different products.

Looking at it on a larger scale, McDonalds and KFC would be indirectly competing for the same reason as stated above. They both supply similar but different products but their products can be used in replacement for the other.

Your aim should be to ensure that you are aware of both the direct and indirect competition which you may face in your Business.

<u>ACTION POINTS</u>

In order to explore your competition, you must carry out an analysis of both your direct and indirect competition. The following exercises will help you do this:

1. Make a list of at least between 5-10 direct competitors and 5-10 indirect competitors for your Business.

2. With each competitor, answer the following questions:

   • What products or services do they supply?

   • How do they deliver their products or services?

   • Who is their target market?

   • What are some of their weaknesses?

STEP 11

EXPLORE YOUR 'SWOT'

"To think creatively, we must be able to look afresh at what we normally take for granted."

GEORGE KNELLER

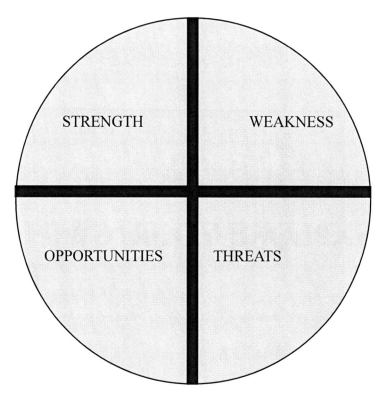

A SWOT analysis is a tool which is used to explore your capabilities both as a Business owner and the capability of your Business as a whole. The SWOT allows you to explore your Business internally and in relation to external factors which may also determine the success of your Business. SWOT stands for:

- Strengths,
- Weaknesses,
- Opportunities
- Threats

The SWOT analysis allows you to examine your Business environment. Your Business environment refers to the factors which affect your company's operations such as customers, competitors, suppliers, distributors, industry trends, regulations, government activities, the economy, demographics, and introduction of new technologies. Therefore a SWOT analysis will help you to determine how effective your new Business will be in relation to these factors and which areas needs to be worked on before embarking on your Business venture.

SWOT analysis shows you the strength of your Business idea, the weaknesses of the idea, the threats that occur from your external environment (i.e. coming from outside your company) and the opportunities which can be exploited to the advantage of your Business idea.

This analysis can be broken down into two sections, the Strength and Weaknesses are those factors which affect the company internally. This means that they are both factors directlyrelate to your Business and can be controlled by you. The next section is the Opportunities and Threats; these are the factors that are not controlled by you as a Business owner but come from external sources such as your competitors, Government laws etc. Let's take a look at these factors one by one:

Strengths

The strengths in relation to your Business refer to those factors and characteristics that could give your Business a competitive advantage in the market. When talking about your strengths, this can be explored in terms of your capability as the Business owner and also the strengths of your Business as a whole. Here are some questions you can ask yourself to determine your strengths:

1. What are your differentiation methods? What makes your Business stand out in the market as a whole? You should already be familiar with this from previous chapters where you looked at differentiating your Business. You need to examine the characteristics which you see as a Business owner that can be used to your advantage for your Business against your competitors. E.g. 'our business is located locally, so we are able to deliver your dry cleaning to you on a same day delivery'.

2. What would the customer see when looking at your Business from the outside? These are the characteristics that can attract a customer to you and make you stand out from other competitors, these are the attributes which your company possess that can impact your customers in a positive way e.g. your customers may say, "I choose to use Upload Web Design company because their staff are very skilled and they give free consultation on how to improve the use of our website."

When talking about the strengths of your company, you need to be realistic; there is no point in being optimistic and talk about attributes which your company does not currently possess. Remember that the main reason for using the SWOT analysis is to examine the current state of your Business idea in relation to these four factors. When you are realistic, then you are able to know which areas are lacking and which areas need to be worked on.

One of the easiest ways to analyse the strength and weaknesses of your Business idea from your point of view as the owner is by using the five factors which were explored in the Capability risks earlier in this book. Here is how you can connect these factors:

- Passion: Your passion could be used as strength and this may apply to Businesses which deliver personal services such as a Youth Confidence Coach. In this instance the coach may refer to his passion for young people as the factor which helps him connect to them in a more intimate way and bring out the confidence in them.

  - Knowledge: Any form of knowledge which you possess or qualifications gained can be used as strength in your Business e.g. We are a team of ACCA accredited accountants which means that we are governed by this body and we are under strict codes of conduct.

  - Experience: This is used by several types of Businesses in gaining competitive edge. For example, estate agents can use the fact that they have been trading for over 90 years as a reason for their expertise in the field.

  - Skills: We've dealt with the issue of using your special skills as the niche in your market. You can state the special skills which you possess as a strength for your Business E.g. if you are running a fashion design company, you could use your ability to hand make some of your designs as a strength.

  - Resources: The resources which your company possess can be used as a strength, e.g. as a printer, you have just acquired a printing machine which enables you to turnover your printing needs on the same day while your competitors take a minimum of 24 hours to do so.

When discussing and thinking about your strengths, it is important to consider you competitors. For example, if all your direct competitors are offering affordable prices for their products, then there will be no point in putting 'affordable prices' as your strength.

Here are some of the other questions that can be considered when looking at your strengths:

- What advantages does your organization have?

- What do you do better than anyone else?

- What unique resources can you draw upon that others can't?

- What do people in your market see as your strengths?

- What is your organization's Niche or USP?

Weaknesses

The weaknesses in your Business are also internal factors which can affect the success of your Business. These simply refer to the attributes and characteristics that can give your company a competitive disadvantage in your industry or market. Again with the weaknesses, it is very important for you to be realistic about your Business idea as the reason for looking at this analysis is to show you the areas where your weak spots are, so they can be dealt with and turned into strengths.

Similar to the strengths, one of the easiest ways to explore your weaknesses is to look at those five factors from your 'Capability Risk' which are, passion, knowledge, experience, skills and resources.

You need to look at what qualifications and or knowledge would be beneficial to your company which you or your staff do not currently possess e.g. an accounting firm should be ACCA regulated so as to make sure that they are following the right practices and this applies to many other professions.

You also need to consider the skills which are required for your Business which you do not currently have. For example, there are certain types of Businesses where you need certain skills in order to operate effectively and staff members need to attend regular trainings either internally or externally in order to be up to date with the skills training.

One of the most important elements to consider when treating the weaknesses in your Business is the resources which you currently possess and those which you need for your Businesses to function effectively. Every type of Business need different resources and previous chapters of this book has dealt with the issue of resources. As previously mentioned, your resources could range from those needed for your premises, those needed to make your Business function etc. The amount of resources needed in order to make your Business function will depend on the type of Business which you are setting up. For example, the tools needed for an IT Support company will be different from that needed for a beauty salon.

Again, consider your weaknesses both from your own point of view and the point of view of your customers. You can examine your weaknesses using two sentences:

1.   What can you see as a weakness in your Business idea?

2.   What could be seen as weaknesses to your potential customers?

Here are some other questions which you may ask yourself when considering the weaknesses of your company:

• What could you improve in your Business?

• What should you avoid?

• What factors could lose you sales?

Remember that it is better to be realistic now and deal with the problems than be overly optimistic and face the problems later in your Business. Your main focus should be how to turn your weaknesses into strengths.

Opportunities

Opportunities are exactly what the word says. Opportunities simply refer to those external factors which may give your Business an advantage. These are those factors which are not within your control but can have an impact on your Business. Opportunities arise in several ways. It could arise as a result of:

✔ A change in a Government legislation

- An introduction of a new technology

- Realising an unfulfilled customer need

- Removal of international trade barriers

- Local events

- Changes in the trend of your target market

- Opportunities created by the weaknesses of your competitors

When looking at the issue of opportunities in the market place for your Business, you need to examine your "Critical Moment". These are the situations which arise and create huge opportunities for your Business. Remember, as we said earlier on, that opportunities and threats are external circumstances which can affect your Business. How these affect your Business will determine whether it is classed as an opportunity or a threat. For example, if you are starting up a company that produces sportswear, a 'critical moment' would be the Olympics. This would create an opportunity for growth for your Business if you link your products to the Olympics. The Olympics would be your critical moment to shine.

Every Business needs to keep an eye out for its critical moment and make the best use of it. For example, the critical moment for a company which provides Business training could be the new Government initiative to increase entrepreneurship among young people in the country. You must see opportunities everywhere and look out for untapped resources.

Another way to spot an opportunity is to examine your competitors and the gaps which they are not filling. As mentioned in earlier chapters, you must know the products and services which your competitors supply and the methods which they use. This will help you in creating an opportunity with gaps that have not been filled and using it to your own advantage by turning it into your 'strength'. Simply put, you can create an opportunity for your Business by looking for weaknesses in your competitors.

Your competitors could either present you with opportunities or threats and you have to seize the opportunities from them. For example, if you are starting up a new Estates Agency in a particular local area, it will be very beneficial to understand the process used by the current participant in that market so you can know the opportunities that can arise for you in the area which you can tap into as you enter the market.

Opportunities will always present themselves and they may arise out of a situation which is out of your control but you can use it to your own advantage. E.g. a networking event can take place in your area which will contain your target market. This is an opportunity for a new Business, therefore all you need to do is attend and use this opportunity to gain new customers, increase your network and gain some new Business. This is why it is important to always keep an eye out for important changes and updates through several media avenues such as the internet, Magazines TV, Radio etc.

Here are some of the questions which you can ask yourself when looking for opportunities in the market:

• What good opportunities can you spot?

• What interesting trends are you aware of?

It is said that "Some people see opportunities where others see problems". As a Business owner, you must always be aware of changes that come about which can impact your company positively. This can either come through the government or other sources. If you are trading in a B2G market, then it is important that you keep track of Government policies and changes as this is bound to affect your Business.

Look out for opportunities that could be turned into your strengths, for example there could be a segment of your market which has not been targeted yet and you can decide to tap into this market and use it as a niche for your Business. There could also be an introduction of a new technology which you could utilise in your Business that could be seen asstrength.

Threats

Threats are the exact opposite of opportunities. These are situations that can arise which would pose a threat to the growth and profitability of your company. Threats are environmental factors which could arise in your industry or market that can affect your Business negatively. These are the situations which are out of your control but can still have an effect on your Business. Such situations can include the following:

✓ Change in your customer taste: Where they do not buy your products as much as they used to. This could be caused by environmental changes such as weather changes. For example, a company which provides package holiday would be aware of the peak seasons for holidays and seasons where customers are less likely to buy from them. You must be aware of circumstances or situations which can cause a change in your customer taste.

✔ Emergence of substitute products in your market: This is one of the factors that can pose the most threat to your Business. A new competitor in the market is most likely to reduce your market share especially if the competitor is a direct one. This means that your profitability and growth will be affected. When this occurs, you can find ways of differentiating yourself in order to stand out from the competition.

✔ New regulations: Just as regulations can bring new opportunities, certain regulations will cause a threat to your Business. You must keep up with changes to Government legislations which would impact your Business negatively.

✔ Increased trade barriers: There are certain barriers which may pose a threat to your Business. Typical examples are introduction of tax or tariffs that are imposed on international trade. You must make sure that you keep an eye out for any barriers which can affect the trading of your products and services.

✔ Economic changes: Economic changes can have a drastic effect on your Business but this will depend on the type of market which you are targeting. E.g. the recession caused a closure of several businesses and this affected those Businesses which were trading especially in the B2B market. The high level of unemployment also means that Businesses trading in the B2C market will be highly affected as it means that customers will have less money to spend on items that are not a necessity.

When looking at the issue of threats in relation to your company. Here are some of the questions which you have to ask yourself:

• What obstacles do you face?
• What are your competitors doing?
• Is changing technology threatening your position?
• Could any of your weaknesses seriously threaten your business?

You need to consider these questions and examine your environment very well, looking for threats to your Business.

The SWOT analysis is not just used for finding out your strengths, weaknesses, opportunities and threats but also to find out areas where your business is likely to be at a disadvantage to its competitors and find ways of tackling those issues. Your main focus after looking at your threats and weaknesses are simply to examine how to overcome these and turn your weaknesses into strengths and overcome the threats that you may face as a Business and turn these into opportunities if possible. As well as looking at the negative impact of this analysis on your Business, you can also look at the positive side of the analysis which are your strengths and your opportunities. The analysis would have exposed the strengths of your company to you, some of these you may have known before, and others you may not have known about.

Once you are able to recognise the opportunities that are available to your out there, the next step is to look at ways of tapping into these opportunities. The same applies to threats, once you realise the threats, you will need to put measures in place to ensure that you can overcome them.

Let's take an Web design company as an example, one of the weaknesses could be the fact that they are unable to offer some types of websites due to lack of appropriate up to date software. One of the ways to overcome this will be to look at the cost of the software required and device a means of acquiring it. You will be surprised at the issues that you will find once you start looking at your Business and exploring the weaknesses that may hinder the growth of your Business. The first step to take is to recognise each weakness and then look for ways to tackle it.

One of the main threats that could be faced by the web design company may be the introduction of 'DIY' website packages on the internet which allows novice computer users to build their own websites at very cheap prices with the availability of several templates. This will mean that people will not be willing to spend more money with a website designer when they can build a site themselves at a very cheap price.

This has given the consumers an alternative to the services of the web design company. The next step to be taken by this company is to look for ways of overcoming this threat. The business owner could decide to offer extra incentives to customers such as added support rather than website development only. The company could decide to offer free consultation to customers with every website which would not be available with the packages sold online. This is added value which could still attract the customers.

The main point is that you need to be constantly aware of the state of your company in terms of the SWOT analysis. This is not something that you do as a one off but an analysis that has to be carried out regularly over a period of time. Situations will always change both internally and externally especially if you are planning for growth within your new Business. You must always be aware of the changes to your company's strength and weaknesses and which attributes of your company has crossed over from being a Strength to a Weakness.

It is also very important that you are aware of the opportunities which can come up for your Business. As a business owner, it is important to continually search for opportunities and one of the ways to do this is to regularly carry out a SWOT analysis. If you plan to take on staff members at the beginning of your Business venture or go into partnership with others, it is important to always keep up to date with the latest developments which can have a positive influence on your company so that you can give a constant update to those involved in the Business.

Regularly carrying out the analysis means that you will not be caught unawares of any threats which may arise in your Business environment, industry or market. This is very important as threats can lead to loss of profits and this can eventually lead to the closure of a Business. You should always be looking for how to use your strengths to maximise every opportunity which arises.

Let's take the same IT web design company as an example again, if one of the strengths of the Business owner is the ability to train and speak very well, he may decide to use this skill as an opportunity to give tips and advice in order to win new clients. He may decide to look for events where he can speak in order to promote himself to a mass audience as an expert in the web design company. The example given is one which highlights how you can use your strengths to take advantage of given opportunities.

Other ways which you can look at the analysis is to examine how you can use your strengths to overcome a threat that comes up in your Business. Threats could appear in different forms and this is why you need to constantly consider all the external factors that can affect our Business as the owner. Whenever you detect a threat against your Business, this could be the financial, legal or any other types of threat, the first thing to think about is what strengths do you possess which can be used to tackle the threats that you face.

As a new Business owner, you will be entering a new market; whether it existed before or you are looking to target an untapped market, it is important that you are aware of the threats which you are likely to face and look at ways which you can tackle these threats using your strengths.

There was a story of a certain large company whose American office was destroyed in the terrorist attack which happened in 2011. When this happened, it was unexpected and there were crucial information contained in the computer systems in the building that was destroyed. Such information included the database of past and present clients and this meant that failure to retrieve these information may have a drastic effect on the company as a whole and can lead to a potential closure of the company.

Due to the careful installation of a backup system for the company data, they were able to immediately retrieve the information from the system and inform all the clients about the disaster. The retrieval of this information meant that the London office were still able to carry on dealing with clients who were being dealt with by the American office and therefore kept the company alive.

This is a perfect example of a situation where a threat occurred against this company but they were able to overcome it using thestrength of the company which was a very knowledgeable head of technical services and a reliable backup system that came into use when needed. Looking at this example, you must always think about how you can utilise your strengths in case you encounter unexpected threats.

ACTION POINTS

Create a table with two rows and two columns. The top two columns should be labelled as your strengths and weaknesses while the bottom two columns should be labelled as your opportunities and strengths.

1. Under the 'Strengths' column, list down all the strengths of your new Business.

2. Under the 'Weaknesses' column, list down all the weaknesses of your new Business.

3. Under the 'Opportunities' column, list down all the opportunities which you can utilise in your new Business.

4. Under the 'Threats' column, list down all the threats that your new Business may face.

5. After writing these down, consider your weaknesses and list down in a separate space ways which you can deal with these weaknesses and possibly turn them into strengths.

6. Look at the threats that your new Business may face and list down the different ways which you can use your strength to combat these threats or even turn them into opportunities Examples have already been given to you above.

STEP 12

SET YOUR PRICES

"The moment you make a mistake in pricing, you're eating into your reputation or your profits."

KATHARINE PAINE

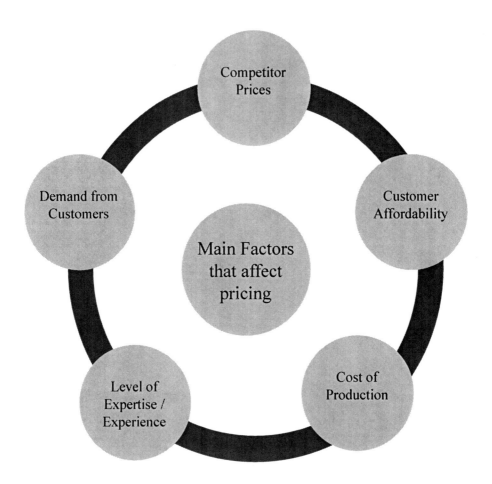

Pricing is another aspect of your Business which you cannot afford to take lightly. Get your prices wrong and your Business could end up shutting down within a short period. Your price does not only have an effect on your company but it sends out a message to your target market. Your pricing contributes to the overall message which you send out about your company.

Your prices will tell your audience how you want your company to be perceived in the market place. For example, the way we would value a company that sells all its items for a pound and another company which sells similar products but at different prices will be different. Your pricing is one of the most important decisions that you can make as a new Business owner. The image you create at the start of your Business is how you will be seen by your customers. For example, if you start off your Business by supplying cheap and affordable products, this is the image which your customers will have of your company as a whole and this may work for or against you, depending on your intended target market.

It's amazing how many Business owners set their prices by basically imitating existing products or 'following the crowd' without taking other factors into consideration before making the decision. You must make sure that you do not fall into this trap. Extensive research must be done before setting the prices for your goods or services and supplying these to your customers.

Not only do your prices affect your company's image and the brand, it can also make or break your company's profitability. One of the main goals of a Business is to make profit and you must consider this before setting prices.

Your pricing strategy will generally depend on several factors. Here are some of them:

The Cost Of Production: Before you can make a decision on your pricing, one of the first factors that you must consider is your total cost of producing your goods or services. If this doesn't happen, then it will spell trouble for the survival of your Business. The best way to do this is to calculate all the costs that will be incurred by your Business. This cost has to include staff, materials, marketing etc (These will be explained further in the next chapters). The price you charge per product or service must cover all the costs that will be incurred in producing that item.

Let's take the web design company as an example, the price which the company will charge for designing a website must cover the costs which will be incurred during the development of the site including staff cost, marketing, materials needed etc. Therefore the typical web design company will charge the customer depending on the hours used in developing the website.

Another example is a company which supplies hair care products. The Business owner must make sure that he covers all the costs that were involved in the production of the items before making the decision on the prices. So the costs which will be taken into consideration will include material costs, labour, shipping etc. if these items were produced in bulk, then the total costs will be divided by the number of products made and this has to be covered in the price charged per item.

Once you have looked at your costs of production, the next step would be to look at the profit margin which you would want on your product or service. For example, if it costs you £50 to produce a particular product, you may sell it for £75 in order to earn £25 profit after all the production costs have been deducted. You should always make a decision on how much profit you want to make after your costs have been deducted, this will help you in choosing the prices to charge for your products or services.

Customer Affordability: Before making a decision on your prices, it is important to carry out a thorough research to find out how much your customers are willing to pay for your products or services. This will be linked to your chosen target market. You must understand your target market enough to know how much disposable income they have which can be spent towards your products or services.

For example, there will be no point in setting a high price for website design which is targeted at small start-ups. They may not necessarily have a lot of funds available at the start-up stage and therefore it will be important to tailor your pricing to your target market and ensure that they are able to afford the prices.

Demand from Customers: It is very obvious that the more demand you have for your products and services, the more flexibility you have on choosing a price. If you have a high demand for your products or service, then you can increase your price without having a detrimental effect on your Business. Likewise, if you find that there's not much demand for your products or services, then you are less likely to charge a high price for them as you would be looking to reduce your price in order to compete in the tight market.

There is however an exception to this rule where a new Business supplies a niche product that doesn't exist in the market at all. Here, the Business owner can still choose the prices regardless of a high demand or not as there are no competitors. An example of this was when 'Apple' invented the IPAD, they could set the prices high as this was an innovative product with no competition at the time.

Competitors Prices: This is one of the most important factors to consider when choosing your prices for your products. You must know the price trends that currently exist in the market. There is no point in charging any price which feels right to you if it's off the mark compared with the existing average in your market or industry.

Before you choose your prices, you must carry out some research into your competitors' position in order to know the prices which they charge for the same items. Once you know how your direct competitors offer the services and the prices they charge, this will make it easy for you to enter your new market and establish yourself.

Level of Expertise / Experience: This will apply more to businesses which supply services more than those that supply goods. When you have established yourself as an expert in your industry, this will tend to generate a high demand for your services. You have already read about how to establish yourself as an expertise in your market in previous chapters. The more skilful you are at your profession, the higher you are able to charge for your services. This can apply to companies such as IT support services, web designs where special skills can help you to increase your prices with your clients.

This can be tied in with experience as the more experienced you are in your Business, the more skilful you will tend to become and the more people will use your services and refer you to others, hence increasing your client base.Experience can also be advantageous when choosing your prices. This can apply where you've got two Businesses that are equally skilled. The only factor that can separate them is the experience which they both have in the industry.

A typical example of this can be seen in the Estates Agency industry. Several Businesses may exist on the high street but the more experienced agencies will tend to charge a higher price than the new ones. Due to their level of experience, they can be trusted more and therefore set their own prices.

Different Pricing Strategies

There are several strategies which you can adopt when deciding on the price of your products or services. As previously mentioned, the strategy which you adopt for your pricing is highly important as a new Business. You strategy can either mean that you fail right from the beginning or you start off with a 'bang'. There are several examples of strategies which are being used by different companies in either introducing new products to the market or introducing a new Business as a whole. Here are some examples of strategies which you can consider when thinking about how to price your products or services:

• The first strategy is known as a penetration strategy which is where companies charge a low price for their products at the start up phase but then start to increase their prices once they have gained a large share of the market. This is quite common among TV subscriptions, telephone subscriptions or general subscriptions companies where you are offered low price to sign up as a new customer and the prices are gradually increased as you become a loyal customer. You can decide to use this strategy if you want to undercut your competitors in the existing market but this has the risk of branding your company as cheap and affordable compared to the competitors and could beperceived as having a lower quality by some in the market.

- The next strategy for pricing is one which is common especially within the electronics suppliers. This is where a company prices its products at a high level when it arrives in the market, but the price is reduced with time. Hence making it available to a wider market. Examples of this can be seen with the launch of new mobile phones, TVs and other electronics which arrive on the shelves at high prices but then reduce the prices gradually as time goes on.

   This type of pricing will depend on your type of Business and the way which you present your brand to your customers. This usually applies to companies that supplies products or goods.

- Another strategy which can be used has already been discussed earlier on; this is where you set your price in relation to your competition. When you look at the average prices charged by your direct competitors, you can either decide to go higher, lower or charge exactly the same price as our competitors.

- You can decide to use the 'cost-plus' strategy where you calculate the total cost of producing the product or services and add a percentage on top as a profit. For example, if it costs you £100 to produce your products, you might decide to make a profit of 20 percent on each item, therefore you will add £20 to the cost of production to make the total price £120. This means that you are aware of your profit margin on each item sold.

   This type of pricing strategy does not give room for a lot of promotions on the items or price reduction as doing this will reduce the profit or may even lead to the Business just breaking even on the item being sold.

- A strategy which is usually common with particular types of companies is known as the 'optional pricing' where you sell 'extras' with your products in order to maximize the turnover on the product or service being sold. This can be found in several types of Businesses but most common with companies that sell brand new cars. They tend to have a standard price for the cars but charge extra for add-ons and this increases the total cost of the car.

   In order to use this type of pricing strategy, you must have some extra options that you can supply to your customers in relation to the products or services which you are already supplying that will give them extra benefit and add to the price of your product or service. Example will be a web design company that charges extra hourly fee for consultation on top of the actual development of the website where they can take the customer through a step by step consultation of understanding their website needs before developing it.

• 'Premium pricing' is a strategy that has become quite familiar. This is where a company decides to set its prices high right from the start in order to reflect its high quality and exclusivity to the product or service. This type of pricing is usually adopted by companies that supply specialist products such as hand woven clothing or one off design goods.

Examples of such companies are Louis Vuitton, Porsche etc. If you are going to adopt this type of strategy, your whole image and brand must project this. You must also make sure that the quality of products or services which you supply gives the customer some value for their money or else this will generate bad publicity for your company which will drive your customers away.

• There is a strategy which is usually adapted by supermarkets where goods are sold in bundles at reduced prices. A typical example of this is the 'Buy One Get One Free' offers or 'Buy Two for the Price of One' offers. This is where you offer promotions on your products or service packages as a bundle.
This type of strategy is usually used by companies to increase sales and also gain customer loyalty. It can also be used by companies such as events companies where they offer two tickets for the price of one to a show in order to fill the seats and increase ticket sales.

These are just some of the strategies which you can choose for your pricing. You can either choose one of them for your new Business or you can chose to explore other methods, the main point is to ensure that whatever strategy you choose, you have a reason for choosing it.

As a new Business, you must consider the fact that you are a new brand either entering an existing market or creating a new market of your own which hasn't been tapped into yet. Therefore, your priority should be to gain maximum exposure for your brand and gaining as much market share as possible on your point of entry.

ACTION POINTS

The first step to take is to choose the pricing strategy which you have decided to use for your Business:

1. From the list given, choose the strategy which you will use in pricing your products or services.

2. If you haven't chosen any of these, define your own strategy.

3. Give a description of how the chosen strategy will be used in your Business.

The next step is to carry out some competitive research:

1. Pick out ten direct competitors who supply the same products or services as you

2. List down all the products or services which you supply.

3. Write down the prices that the ten competitors charge for each of your products or services.

Finally, state your own prices:

1. Make a list of all your products or services and write the price which you will charge at the start-up phase next to each item.

STEP 13

CREATE YOUR ELEVATOR PITCH

"I feel that luck is preparation meeting opportunity."

OPRAH WINFREY

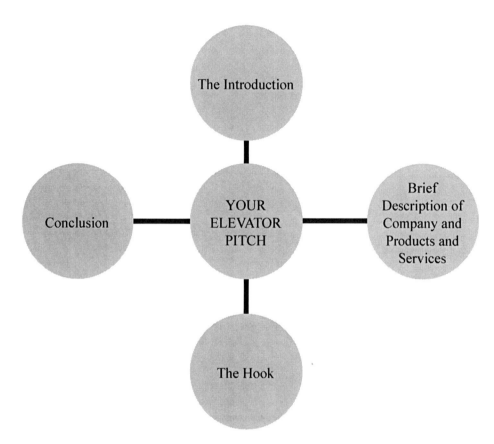

As a new Business owner, one of the most important attributes to possess is the ability to sell yourself and your Business. You must have the ability to confidently present your Business concept to others even if it's the first thing in the morning. The same thing applies to your members of staff, but you must make sure as the Business owner that you are able to effectively communicate the whole concept of your Business to anyone who requests it.

The ability to sum up your Business and the services or products which you supply in under a minute is a skill which many Business owners don't tend to work on. It's amazing how you will meet people at networking events, at social events, family occasions and other places and ask them a simple question:

"So what do you do for a living?"

The answers that you get will tell you whether the individual has actually taken time out to work on their elevator pitch. This is very crucial especially when you are a new Business owner on the hunt for your first client. If I ask you to tell me about your Business and you are unable to clearly define the concept behind your Business as clear as possible and broken down in the simplest and understandable form, you have either lost a potential customer, referral or investor.

An 'elevator pitch' is a quick summary of what your company does and the whole concept of your Business, presented in a way that excites the listener and keeps them wanting to know more. Imagine this scenario, you enter an elevator and you are standing next to someone who has the potential of putting a huge investment into your Business which can turn it around massively. This is a chance of a life time that you can't afford to miss. The only problem is that you only have the length of the lift ride to make your mark on the investor. This means that you only have less than a minute, usually, to speak and make your impression. This is where a well rehearsed pitch comes in play.

Your elevator pitch is not just a crammed down version of your Business plan, nor is it a boring narration of your Business idea. Rather, it is an exciting and captivating overview of your company and one which is likely to capture the attention of the listener. Elevator pitches tend to be very short as they sometimes don't last up to a minute. Of course this is not only restricted to being used in an elevator, it can be used at events, when meeting potential clients, pitching to investors or describing your Business to any member of the general public who can be a potential source of referral.An elevator pitch is a concise, carefully planned and well rehearsed description of your company and its products and services. As mentioned earlier, this must be very understandable so that even someone with no business knowledge or knowledge of your industry should be able to understand it in the time it takes to ride up an elevator.

One of the worst situations you can find yourself in is where you are trying to tell someone about your Business and the person loses interest in the conversation.

This is what happens when you do not have a well practised pitch. In previous chapters, I have stated that word of mouth marketing is the most effective form of advertising and you cannot create promoters of your products and services if they do not have an understanding of the concept themselves.

The elevator pitch can come handy in various situations and circumstances, it can be used for:

- Attracting potential investors to your Business: As previously mentioned, you may get an opportunity to pitch your Business concept to a potential investor in a very short period of time.

- Hooking in potential customers to your Business: You could meet potential clients in unexpected circumstances and having a practiced pitch will help you to effectively introduce your product or service.

- Group introductions: You may get the chance to introduce yourself at group meetings to people who could potentially become a source of referrals for you.

- Individual introductions: This can happen in any given situation where a friend, colleague or family member introduces you to someone else and you are asked what you do. You never know who the person is connected to and the impact they can have on your Business.

- Trade Fairs andNetworking events: If you are a Business owner who regularly visits trade shows, exhibitions and networking events, the elevator pitch is a 'must know' for you as you will always meet people at these events who are eager to know about you and your Business.

- Social Events: You will always find someone who asks about your profession or Business at social gathering, this can be in a bar, restaurant or parties. You may even be in a queue at the airport and you only have the length of that queue to pitch your Business concept to the person standing in front of you who can potentially impact your Business.

These are only some examples of situations where elevator pitches can come into use but you must be ready to use it at any given situation. Your Business concept must constantly be on 'the tip of your tongue'. Of course you have to understand that the pitch may need a little tweaking for every situation, for example, the type of information which you will focus on when speaking to an investor is different to that which you will emphasise on when speaking to a customer. No matter what the situation is, your aim must always be to capture the attention of the listener.

After going through the process of creating your Business identity in earlier chapters, the issue of creating your Elevator pitch should not be a big one at all. When putting your pitch together, there are two main things that you need to keep in mind:

"It's not just what you say that matters but also how you say it."

Here are some tips to keep in mind when putting together your elevator pitch:

1. **Keep It under 60 seconds:** As mentioned earlier, it is called an elevation pitch because you have little time to deliver it: around 60 seconds. Sometimes even 30 seconds, depending on the situation. Keep your pitch as short as possible, covering the most important points that you need to put across. You might only have that lift ride duration or just a walk down a hallway in order to deliver the pitch so you must keep it as short as possible and most importantly under 60 seconds.

2. **Be Prepared:** There are some opportunities that will only come your way once in a lifetime and others once every couple of years. When you get an opportunity to pitch yourself and your company, you must make sure that you make the best use of it. It's said that "Success happens when preparation meets opportunity", so make sure that you prepare yourself, ready to deliver a great pitch when needed. As a new Business, you will face opportunities to pitch for new Business opportunities, contracts and other types of opportunities; therefore you must make your elevator pitch a top priority.

3. **Keep it Up to Date:** Every business grows and changes over time and you need to make sure that your pitch is kept up to date with every change that occurs in your Business. Whenever a change occurs in your Business, it shouldn't only affect things like your logo, brand etc. but you should also make sure that your pitch is updated and every other member of your company is informed of the changes. Introducing an outdated Business concept to a potential client will project a bad image of your company especially when it's coming from the Business owner.

4. **Create Excitement and spark interest:** As mentioned earlier, it is important that your pitch creates excitement and sparks interest from the listener. You are supposed to hook your listener into your conversation, whether it is an investor or a potential customer. The person must 'want to know more' after you have delivered your pitch. Knowing your company and your products or services is one thing, but having the ability to convey the same message to someone else in an exciting manner is a different skill that has to be practised.

5. **Use a Hook:** As previously mentioned, it is important to make the first few

seconds of your pitch interesting and exciting so that you can keep the listener interested. The best way to do this is by having a hook. A hook is basically a statement or question that grabs the attention of the listener to want to hear more about your Business. Let's take examples of two pitches:

a. "Hi, I'm John Smith, Owner of Upload Graphics Company; we design and print graphic materials."

b. "Hi, I'm John Smith, Owner of Uploads Graphics Company, we design and print graphics materials such as leaflets, Business cards, posters, banners and other marketing materials to help companies represent their brand effectively. We designed the main banners for the Notting Hill Carnival this year and we have designed banners for international airports in the past.

There is a huge difference between these two statements above. Even though they both describe what the company does, one of them is bound to catch your attention even if you are not interested in the services which John Smith is offering.

The second statement will immediately catch your attention and makes you want to hear more about John Smith and his company. The accomplishments attached to the statement have been used to hook in the listener. You can either use a recent achievement, a funny story or a catchy line with your elevator pitch. The main point is that it must captivate the listener.

6. **Pitch yourself, not your idea:** There is a saying that goes:

"People buy from people they trust and like".

As a business owner, your main focus when meeting people is to sell yourself before thinking about selling your Business to the listener. I'm sure you've probably been in a situation where you are standing in front of someone and you lose interest while they are chatting away because you have not 'warmed up' to them.

When people like you, they would want to know more about you and hear what you have to say. Make sure that you highlight your achievements or skills during the pitch. As a start-up, you will find that your initial Business idea is likely to change as time goes on but once you have been able to connect with someone, you will always develop a relationship with the individual no matter the change to your Business concept.

7. **<u>Don't forget to state your need</u>:** This is particularly important for pitching to investors or people who can make an impact in your Business. As a start-up, there may be several needs that you have for your new Business; this could be in terms of finances, resources or expertise. You must always remember to end the pitch with something that you need. This can be tailored to the person you are having the conversation with. You could end by stating the types of clients you would be looking for, or if it is an investor, you will end by stating the amount of money needed as investment. Don't get caught up in other things so that you forget to state what you need.

8. **<u>Don't overwhelm your listener with technical or statistical jargon</u>:** One of the worst experiences you could encounter is where someone speaks to you with technical jargon that makes no sense to you at all. It is important that you keep your pitch very simple and straight to the point. It is also important to tailor your pitch to the environment and the listener; for example, an investor will want to know some statistical figures and facts while an individual in a restaurant may not be interested in those things. So make sure you are aware of the content to include when using your elevation pitch on different occasions.

9. **<u>Practice, Practice, Practice</u>:** This is probably one of the most important tips out of all the ones given in this chapter. There is a famous saying that goes, "Practice Makes Perfect". You must make sure that you rehearse your elevator pitch over and over again so that you do not mess up when the opportunity arises to use it.

10. **<u>Confidence</u>:** Confidence is linked with practice. The more you practise something, the more confident you will become at it. The same principle applies to elevator pitches. Your confidence grows as you practise it in your own time. People can tell whether you are confident or not. Your confidence is always projected in different ways when you are giving a presentation or simply talking. Learn from experiences, listen to feedback and use it to improve your delivery. Confidence shows that you believe in what you are talking about.

11. **<u>Listen</u>:** When engaging in a conversation with someone, it is important to listen to what the other person is saying. If you are not careful, you will be so focused on delivering the pitch that you will not give the listener an opportunity to ask questions. When this happens, you lose the attention of the listener. Listening is as equally important as speaking.

These are just some of the tips which can help you deliver a great elevator pitch at any given time. Your elevator pitch can be broken down into different parts therefore understanding each individual part will help you in putting together a great pitch. Here are some of the components:

Introduction

This is the first part of your elevator pitch. It should contain information such as:

• Your name

• Your role

• Name of your company.

This section can contain a little information about you but you must make sure that you keep it short as you still have to talk about your company and products and services in more detail.

Brief Description of Company and Products and Services:

After introducing yourself and the name of your company, the next thing you need to do is give a little description about what you do and the products and services which you offer. This is one of the most important parts of the pitch. One thing that you must remember, as previously stated above, is to ensure that it is very easy for your listener to understand your company and its products. The worst thing you could do is explain your products and services to a novice in your industry using all the technical terminologies, presuming the person can understand them.

You must find a way to describe your company so that the listener does not get confused and switch off. There is no formula which can be used to describe your company in an easy way but the best way to do this is to practise and try it out with several people and get their response. When describing your company, here are some points you may want to focus on:

• What values does your products or services offer?

• How customers will use your product?

• Mention one or two competitors and sate what makes you better and different. (This must be done very quickly without going into much detail.)

It is also important to perfect your company description until you are sure that it can be understood by a novice because you need to create promoters among people you meet. 'Your promoters' refer to those people who are able to refer your products or services to other people. One thing you always have to remember is that you never know who's connected to the person in front of you in the queue or the person standing next to you in the bar, so always be ready to present your elevator pitch effectively.

The Hook

As mentioned already, your hook is something that grabs the attention of your listener which makes them want to hear more about you and your Business. The hook can prolong the pitch and take it out of the elevator or it can cut the pitch short and lose the attention of the listener. An example of a hook has already been given earlier in this chapter.

A hook can be one of the following:
- An interesting event that's occurred which is linked to your Business. E.g. did you hear about the London riots that destroyed lots of Businesses?

- An achievement or accomplishment by your company that was recognised

- A need that is very evident in the market which your company is solving.

- A very popular line or humorous statement that is linked to your company.

- Sales figures or success stories from your work so far.

These are just examples of your hook. You have to decide which hook you want to use for your pitch. You have to think about what makes your Business idea so fascinating and interesting that anyone would be drawn into the idea.

If you are speaking to a potential investor, they would always want to hear some type of success story, whether in the form of sales to date or number of customers attracted since starting the Business. Of course if you are just starting off your company, then you will need to either talk about reason for starting your company or any sales you made. As a start up, you can always test your products or services with friends, families or others who are willing to try it. You may then use these free trials as testimonials which can then be used as hooks.

One thing you must not do with your hook is lie. Never use information that is not true or yet guaranteed. This will only cause you more problems later when given the chance to present your full Business plan. Do not talk about sales deals which have not yet gone through in the hope that you will get them.

The Conclusion

The conclusion is the part where you state what you would like from the person towhom you are speaking. This can either be in the form of financial investment, referral to a client, resources, partnership or special skills.

This is where the listener has to weigh the first two part of the pitch against your requirement. For example if you were asking for financial investment, the investor would have listened to your hook and listened out for sales to date or interest in your products or services. Your hook is very important to the conclusion, as it determines whether the listener wants to continue speaking after the conclusion or walks away without asking any further questions. When you meet someone, your first thought should be.

"What can he or she offer me?"

That will help you determine how to lay out your pitch.

After finishing your elevator pitch, one of the signs that you've done well is if the listener starts asking questions about you or your Business. This means that they are interested in knowing more. The questions could be directed towards your products or services, Business model, financial figures etc. Therefore you must be ready to answer the questions asked or it can make you seem incompetent. Here are some of the popular questions you may encounter.

- How does the Business model work?
- How would you make money from this?
- Who are your target customers?
- What makes you different from your competitors?
- How will the money be spent (if it is an investment)?
- Where is your breakeven point?

Remember that elevator pitches can vary depending on the situation at hand so be prepared to add and remove one or two things and tailor it to the listener in any given situation.

ACTION POINTS

After learning about the different ways of creating an elevator pitch, the next step is to create yours. Using the examples and explanation given above:

1. Write out your introduction
2. Write down the description of your products / services
3. Write down your Hook
4. Write down your conclusion

Now PRACTISE!

STEP 14

FIND YOUR SOURCE OF FINANCE

"A business that makes nothing but money is a poor business."

HENRY FORD

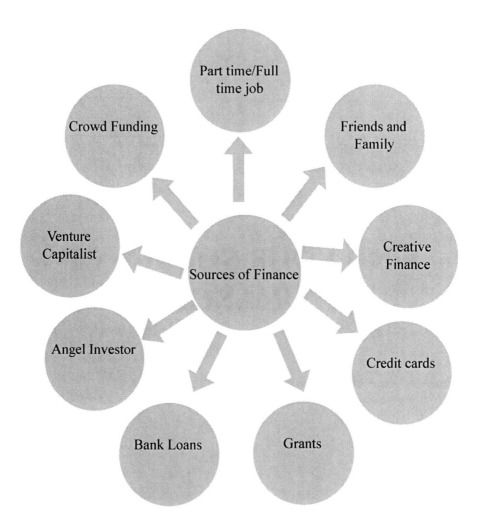

When I get approached by individuals who have an idea, one of the most common obstacles for not taking the idea to the next level is lack of capital. It is true that a level of capital is needed to start a Business but it is important to look at different ways of overcoming this obstacle. One of my favourite quotes is:

"Without money, the dream dies"

Whether you are a small, one man Business starting from your bedroom or a small Business renting an office to start from, you will need some amount of money to start your Business. You need to consider this before stepping out into the Business world and making your idea a reality. One of the biggest mistakes new Business owners make is that they do not consider all the resources or costs which will be incurred in their new Business endeavour and consider the sources of income or finance that can be used in paying for the cost. This only leads to the Business starting off in a bad financial state.

As a new Business owner, it is important for you to get into the habit of keeping a record of your finances (How to do this will be explained in the next chapter). Every Business has a different start up cost and this depends on several factors such as your location, type of premises, resources needed, marketing materials etc., but the key is for you to know your own costs. This will aid you in developing your forecasts and understanding how much finance you need to get your Business off the ground.

Knowing your start up costs is important in starting your new Business as this will help you in putting together your financial plans and forecasts which will in turn give you an idea of when you can make back the money invested. Another common problem with new Entrepreneurs is that they tend to ignore certain costs that are required to make a successful start in their market. When you do this, you will find your Business struggling to take off in the right direction.

For example, you could decide to cut down on your marketing and advertisement due to lack of funds. What may then happen is that you have a great product or service but your customers are unable to see it. Therefore it is important to examine all aspects of your Business and work out a plan for funding or financing the costs.

No matter how small the cost is, it is important that you note it down as it can accumulate to become a bigger number and small numbers tend to make big differences at the end of a financial year where all the costs are adding up or it can come into play when valuing your Business. There are certain factors which will affect the cost of starting your new Business, here are some of them:

- **Business Location:** It is important to note that your location will determine the cost of running your Business. A busy city centre location will potentially cost more than running your Business from a quiet area. Costs such as your Business rates, Rent etc. may be higher in a city centre rather than a quiet area of your city. Thesocial class of the customers located in your Business area may also affect the cost of operating from there.

- **Type of Business:** The cost of running different types of Businesses will obviously differ. Trading on e-bay will most likely cost you less that opening up a new restaurant. There are factors that will cut down the costs such as distribution, marketing etc. You must find out the cost involved with starting your type of Business.

- **Resources needed:** It goes without saying that the resources needed to start your Business will accumulate to form your total cost. Different Businesses require different types of equipments to make their Business run effectively. The equipments needed by an IT consultant will differ from that needed by a new restaurant.

- **Size of Your Business:** The size of your new Business will also affect your Business start-up costs. The bigger the Business, the more resources will be needed to run it. For example, a one man Business will be cheaper to run than a Business running from a commercial office space employing a number of staff. Bear this in mind when deciding on the size of your Business.

As previously mentioned, the most important thing is to ensure that you fully understand the costs that are associated with your own Business. When putting together the different costs in your new Business, here are some of the costs you may need to explore:

- **Production Costs:** These are simply the cost of producing the products which you aim to sell to your customers. They may be direct or indirect costs. For example for a restaurant which sells fast food, there are certain costs involved with production of the food being sold. These costs could involve, raw materials, shipping costs from manufacturer or distributor, manufacturing equipments, packaging, the actual preparation of the food, etc. Your production costs will depends on the type of products which you are supplying.

- **Cost of sales:** The cost of sales will differ from the cost of production because the cost of sales pertains to the costs involved with distribution of your products or services to your customers. They are the costs which you take on as a result of getting your services or products into the hands of the customers. This could be shipping costs, shipping insurance,   Product inventory, warehousing etc. You will find that this could interlink with cost of production in some types of Business but the main focus is not really under which category you place a particular cost but making sure that you do not leave out any cost.

- **Professional and legal fees:** Professional fees are those fees which are paid to professionals to carry out a particular work for you. This could include solicitors, accountants, architects etc. Your professional fees will vary according to the needs of your Business. For example, you could choose to open a retail shop front, with this type of premises you will need a builder, architect and a solicitor to provide professional services for you. As a new Business start-up, there are some legal fees which you may encounter for starting your Business. These may include Partnership agreements, lease agreement for your Business premises, setting up the legal structure for your Business such as your articles of association, trademark registration, patents, copyright, Non - disclosure agreements and some other agreements that may be needed for your Business. This will vary according to the type of Business you want to develop. Apart from legal fees, there are other professional fees that you may need to keep in mind such as your Accountant's fee. Some companies choose to have an ongoing accounting support which means that this will form part of your monthly expenses.

• **Technology or Equipment costs:** As we have mentioned before, every Business has its own types of equipment required. An online company being operated from a living room will require different types of equipments from a retail store with a shop front. Examples of equipments could be computers, mobile phones, printers and any other equipment needed for running your Business. Apart from equipments, there are several technological costs that may be involved in starting your Business, for example, with the new digital age, it is imperative for every company to own a website and have an online presence. Other costs include internet access, servers or network, Computer Internet security etc.

• **Administrative costs:** These are the costs which you will incur on a regular basis while running your Business. These can vary depending on the type of Business. Your administrative costs will be tailored to your particular Business so you need to figure out what they will be for your Business. Examples of these include office supplies. Your office supplies will vary and this is where you need to break them down, even something as little as a stapler must be listed down in your costs. They could include folders and files, cabinets, printing papers, pens, flipcharts etc.

• **Building / Premises Costs:** These are the costs involved with the use of your premises for your Business. As stated in previous chapters, there are several ways of acquiring your Business premises and the costs involved will be determined by the type of premises which you acquire. It is important to note that just because you choose to run your Business from home doesn't mean that you may not have any premises cost. For example, while you are running your

Business from home, you will be using an amount of electricity, internet and other utilities. You will need to account for these in your costing. If you use the same utilities which you use for Business for personal use as well, then you will need to work out the percentage of the total bills which apply to your Business and those which apply to your personal use. An example of this is given below:

$$Business\ Charges = \frac{Total\ hours\ used\ for\ Business\ \ x\ \ Total\ amount\ of\ Bill}{Total\ Hours\ included\ in\ Bill}$$

Your total electricity for the month = £40

Total hours in a month = 24 hours * 30 days = 720 hours

Total hours spent on Business in the month = 240 hours

Total electricity charge for your Business in the month = 240 / 720 * £40 = £13.33

The formula used above can be used to calculate any of your utilities. The point is that you must know how much your utilities will cost you even if you are working from home and learn how to separate this from your personal charges. Examples of Building costs include Business rates, Building insurance, Deposit for acquiring premises, Rent or lease amount, License and permits, parking fees and any other costs associated with getting your premises.

• **Marketing costs:** Your marketing costs are all the costs incurred in reaching your target market. This includes advertising, promotion, public relations etc. Your marketing costs will include design and printing of fliers, business cards, stationary etc. Cost of advertising will also be included in this such as newspaper advertising, internet advertising etc. Your marketing also includes any events or shows which you use for promoting your Business and if you take on any sponsorship opportunities. Your Business will have its own marketing strategies and as we have dealt with earlier, you will have to know which strategies your new Business will be utilizing and the costs involved. This category basically covers all the costs that aid you in marketing your Business.

• **Staff and Employees:** These are the costs which are involved with hiring of staff. As mentioned earlier, your Business may not need to hire staff at the beginning so this may not apply to you or you could decide to pay yourself as an employee of the company, whatever route you choose to go through, you must list down all the costs involved whether it isabout hiring yourself or taking on staff members. These costs include salaries, taxes, benefits, insurance, compensation, bonuses or recruitment costs to agencies etc.

These are just some examples of cost categories which you may come across while thinking about your start-up costs. As I have mentioned, you may add your own categories or arrange your costs however you wish but the main focus is to ensure that you break down your costs in an understandable method both to you and anyone who may be interested in looking at your figures.

<u>ACTION POINTS</u>

After looking at the different categories of costs that may be involved in setting up a new Business, the next step is for you to apply this to your Business:

1. List down all the different cost categories as stated above

2. Add any other category which hasn't been mentioned which you may find suitable for your costs.

3. For each category, create a table with two columns. The first column will contain the different items under the category and the second column will contain the cost of each item. For example under the Building / Premises category, the items may include Building rent deposit, One year rent etc.

4. After putting the items for each category and their costs, calculate the total costs for each category.

During my coaching profession, I have met many individuals who have approached me about their ideas. One of the first questions which I ask is their start-up budget. You will be shocked to hear the range of figures which I get. I've had individuals who have approached me who claim that their new Business will cost them £900 000 to start up and a few years later, they start the same Business with under £10000. The problem that most aspiring Business owners have is that they do not accurately define their start-up costs and some tend to exaggerate the costs included in the budget.

One of the basic fundamentals of a Business start up is simple; if you don't have the funding or finances to get the Business off the ground properly, you won't go very far. Once you understand the costs involved in starting your new Business, the next step is to look at the different ways of securing the funding needed.

Your aim is to ensure that you start your Business in the most effective way without compromising on the necessities that will contribute to the success of your Business. One of the methods which can be adopted is the Bootstrapping method. Bootstrapping simply means starting and running your Business without external capital but from personal finances. This means that you start your Business without the use of bank loans or investment. It can include the help of other people such as family members etc. Here are some of the advantages of the bootstrapping method:

• Using your own money to start your Business gives you the freedom to make your own decisions as a Business owner.

  • You do not incur any debts from the start of your Business.

  • You do not spend years trying to raise the needed investment for your Business.

  • Using your money means that you are more likely to work harder to make the Business successful and you will be more involved in the day to day running of the Business.

When you choose the bootstrap method for starting your Business, it means that you have to develop a system whereby you can 'start small but think big'. Your main focus would be to cut costs where possible and ensure that you do not overspend. Let's look at some of the methods you can use for financing your new Business when bootstrapping:

1. **Part-Time Jobs:** Many start up Business owners tend to start running their Businesses while they are still in a part time job or some even maintain a full time job and start funding the Business from the start up phase until it is providing enough income to sustain itself. One of the mistakes that you can make as a new Business owner is to totally depend on the Business to fund itself from the beginning without taking the costs involved into consideration. This could work for some types of Businesses especially those which are skill based e.g. masonry or plumbing where there are potentially less start-up costs. You must make sure that you have enough finance to sustain your Business start up till it's able to sustain itself. Taking on a part time job is one way to do this. This means that you will not need to pay yourself as an employee at the beginning and you can focus on putting any income made from your Business back into building and growing the Business. There are several types of part time jobs which you can take on in order

to sustain your Business, these include weekend jobs, evening jobs, or night jobs.

2. **Friends and family:** This is one of the routes which many ignore when looking for start-up finance for their new Business. When you have a great idea, your first point of contact should be those around you who may help fund the idea. One thing which is very essential and applies to most types of funding is to have a good Business plan. For anyone to consider investing in your Business, they must make sure that you are able to give them a return on their investment. Friends and family are always a good source of investment as they do not tend to incur interest over time except if it is agreed between both parties. With friends and family, it is not as formal as the other forms of investment but you can ensure that you are protected by drafting out a contract to show the terms of the lending in order to avoid any problems arising in the future.

3. **Creative Finance:** This type of financing fits in perfectly with the Bootstrapping ideology. It must be said though that this method does not work very well with every type of Business. An example of creative financing is where you can ask your customers to pay in advance while you supply the products or services. This can apply to a Business such as a web designer who asks the customers to pay in advance and builds the website for them after payment is made. Another way to be creative is also by convincing your suppliers to supply you goods on credit and agree to pay by a particular date. The main point of creative financing is to make the Business fund itself. You have to find ways of being creative. You do have to be careful though when going through this route as it means that you must put every cost of running your Business into consideration.It also means that you depend on the Business acquiring customers in order to run effectively.

Apart from Bootstrapping, you can also decide to go through different funding routes which involve the investment of outsiders' money into your start-up. Here are some examples:

1. **Credit Cards:** Many individuals turn to their credit cards in order to fund their new Businesses. This is one of the ways which you can make sure you keep control of the payments on the money owed. You must be careful when taking this approach and also ensure that you are aware of the APR on your credit card so you don't end up in more debt than you can handle. The danger with taking this route is that you will depend on the company making money in order to pay back the money owed on the credit card except if you have a part time job which pays off the debt on the credit card.

2. **Bank Loans:** If you are an established company with a good credit rating, a

lot of money in your Bank account, lots of experience in your Business industry and a good Business plan, it is quite easy to acquire a loan from the banks to fund your new Business. When you are a new Business Start up with no previous industry experience, it becomes harder to approach the banks. It is not impossible to get a bank loan but it means that you have to prepare yourself adequately before approaching the banks. You will be asked a lot of questions and you must be prepared for this as the banks have to make sure that you can pay back the money you are requesting. When you are approaching the bank, there are two main questions you must be able to answer. They are:

- *How much do you want to borrow?*

- *How are you going to pay it back?*

These are the questions which the lender would want to know as they will determine whether they would consider giving you a chance or not. Some banks may ask for collateral against the loan and others may not. The lenders will assess the risks associated with giving you the loan and this is where you have to make sure you can prove to the lender that there is a low risk of lending you the money. When you are going into a meeting with a lender, here are some of the questions which you can ask yourself in preparation:

⇨   How much do I need? You must have a figure in mind .Calculate all your predicted costs and add some money on top of it just to cover any unseen expenses.

⇨   How am I going to use the money? The lender will also ask you this question. You do not want to tell a lender that you want a loan in order to pay yourself; these generally tend to be declined. Loans are generally used to pay off debts in your Business, pay for your operating costs, or cover all other costs of your Business.

⇨   When will I be able to repay the loan? Your Business plan should show your potential break-even point where you are able to start making back the money invested in the Business. You must be able to show the lender this information as this will let them know the viability of your Business.

⇨   What Collateral have I got? As previously mentioned, lenders may ask for collateral as lending is a risk. You should think about something that can be used against the loan in case of any problem. This will help with convincing the banker.

In addition to asking yourself these questions, here are some of the factors which can affect your ability to get a loan for your new Business:

a. **Business Plan:** This is the most important piece of information needed before approaching a lender for a loan. A good and comprehensive Business plan makes a big difference in the eyes of the lender. It shows your seriousness and commitment towards the long term goal of your Business. A good Business plan will also show the lender the viability of your Business and the chances which they have of making a good return on their investment.
A business plan will support your application with back –up figures and information needed such as your marketing strategies. Getting a loan can be a very tough task for a new Business and this is why you must make sure your Business plan is very comprehensive. You may need to check it over with a friend or trusted colleague before approaching the lender.

b. **Type of Business:** The type of Business which you are starting may also influence your chances of getting a loan. Some Businesses have higher risks than others and there are Businesses with more requirementsfrom lenders than others. For example a new Start up has a higher risk than an established Business.

c. **Personal Credit History:** As the individual requesting the loan, you will need to prove your ability to pay back the money requested. If you have a bad credit history, this will not help your loan application. In this case, you may need to put up a collateral security with your application which just secures the loan in case of future problems. It is important for you to know the state of your credit score before approaching a lender as this will prepare you for any issues that may arise.

d. **Length of Time in Business:** Your experience in your chosen industry may also affect your chances of getting the loan. The lender will look at your Business experience and industry experience. Once you have been able to sustain your Business through a three to five year period, your chances of getting a loan increases whereas a start up may find it more difficult to apply for a loan.

e. **Your Business Structure:** Your type of Business structure may also affect your application for a loan. This refers to the legal structure of your company i.e. how it was incorporated. If you are running your Business as a sole proprietorship, you may have a lower chance of getting a loan than a company which runs as a limited company with shares. This is another factor to bear in mind but each lender will have their specific criteria.

These are just some of the factors which can affect your loan application. There are others which have not been mentioned such as the interest rate, the state of the banking system etc. You need to consider all of these factors before thinking about going for a loan.

3. <u>Grants:</u> There are several types of Government grants which are available to Business start-ups and you need to find out which ones are available at different times. For example, there are grants which are available to young adults starting new Businesses through different organisations and charities such as the Princes Trust. There are also other funding bodies that are able to offer grants to Businesses such as the Lottery Fund. You must find out which one applies to your Business criteria. These grants usually have their own criteria to qualify for them.

4. <u>Angel Investor:</u> An angel investor is a wealthy individual; who is looking to invest in a company at the start-up phase and in exchange for the investment will take an ownership in the Business. An example of this is seen on the popular TV show titled 'Dragons Den'. Angel investors are becoming more popular. More and people seem to have money in the bank which they want to invest in better opportunities as long as there is a good Business plan and proven market place. With angel investors, you are likely to get a low interest rate and therefore this may be a better option compared to applying to a bank loan.

Angel investors tend to either invest financially into your Business or input both their money and skills for a share of the company. This can vary depending on the investor. Angel investors tend to be former or current entrepreneurs themselves, so you are bound to get more than just a monetary investment from them. Do keep in mind that angel investors invest in your company expecting a return and growth in the Business, therefore they are likely to have some 'hands on' decision making in the company as they now have a vested interest in your company and its success.

One way to find angel investors is to search for investor meet-up groups which have developed in several areas where investors meet regularly to hear pitches from start-ups with the need for funding in their new ideas.

5. <u>Venture capitalists:</u> Venture capital is another way to finance your new Business. It is a term used for investors who buy part of a company. The aim of a venture capitalist is to buy some shares or equity in a company which has a promise of growth or success. A venture capitalist prefers to invest in high risk and high growth companies which are likely to give a high return on their shares. Venture capitalists will usually invest for a period of five to seven years and they will usually want a return on their money either through the sale of the whole company or by offering to sell their shares of the company to the public in the future.

Apart from acquiring a percentage of the company in return for their investment, a venture capitalist may also want to have a position on the company's board of directors as this means they are able to monitor and have an input in the success of the company. Always remember that a venture capitalist is very much interested in making a rich return on the investment and can decide to sell his or her shares in order to pull out.

6. <u>Crowd Funding:</u> Crowd funding is where you acquire the finances needed for your start up from various people. The whole idea of crowd funding is to collect small amounts of money from either friends or family members which will in turn make up the collective amount needed for your Business.

For example, if your Business requires £5000 start-up finance, you may choose to approach 20 family members to give £250 each towards your idea in order to reach the total figure. There are several websites which encourage crowd funding and can be used to collect the funds needed from several individuals.

The great thing about crowd funding is that you may find many individuals who will donate towards your idea without asking for anything back in return as long as you are not asking for a substantial amount. You may also find other individuals who will ask for equity or their investment back at some point in the future.

These are just some of the methods which you can adopt for financing your Business. You can find other ways which are not listed above. Different methods are always being introduced to help start-ups, especially with the introduction of different technologies. You must look out for new funding avenues.

ACTION POINTS

As mentioned above, there are several avenues of funding your Business. Some have already been given to you while there may be others which haven't been mentioned.

1. Set yourself a challenge of finding five other funding avenues that can be used which haven't been mentioned above.

2. Looking at your start-up costs, list down all the avenues you can use for acquiring the finances which you need from the different options.

3. If you have chosen more than one source of funding, write down how much you will acquire through each avenue.

STEP 15

KNOW YOUR NUMBERS

"There are plenty of ways to get ahead. The first is so basic I'm almost embarrassed to say it: spend less than you earn."

PAUL CLITHEROE

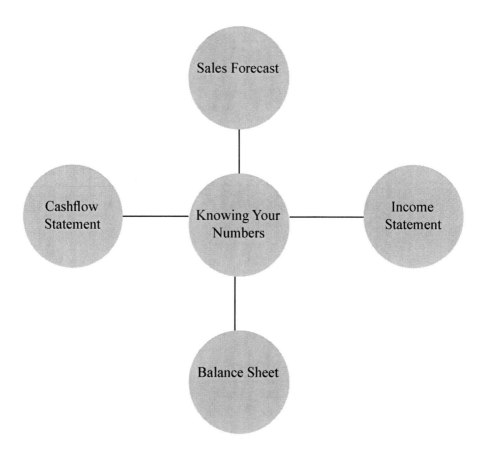

As a new Business owner, you must cultivate the right habits and practices from the start. One of the fundamental principles which you must hold on to is to keep track of your cashflow. Your cashflow refers to the movement of money in and out of your Business. It is the way your finances are managed in your Business. This simply means that you are able to track the money which your company makes and measure it against the outgoings in your company.

A Business owner who doesn't keep a track of their cashflow regularly will probably not be in Business for a long time. As a new start-up Business, you must cultivate a habit of keeping a record of your cashflow and monitoring it while your Business is still young so that you can get used to this habit as your company grows. There are many companies which end up in a huge financial trouble as the company grows larger due to lack of regularly monitoring the cashflow of the company.

As mentioned earlier in this book, the main aim of your Business is to ensure that you are making profit. In order to do this, your sales must exceed your spending or cost hence, the importance of keeping a record of your cashflow.

Existing Business owners tend to rely heavily on their accountants to manage the finances of their companies and keep track of their daily cash flow, depending on the size of the company. Although it is essential that you have an Accountant in place for your company as it grows, you must remember, as a new Business owner, that you have a responsibility of making sure that your company is in a good financial position and the cash flow is kept on the positive side. This means that there is profit generated regularly. If you are intimidated by numbers and figures, there are lots of very good affordable software available on the internet as well as other ways to keep track of your numbers without the need of an accountancy degree. As you start trading and your company gets bigger, you can employ an accountant who can then manage your finances for you.

The reality is simply that you do not need an accountancy degree or have an in depth understanding of accounting in order to keep track of the most important numbers to your company as a Business owner. There is no excuse for you as a Business owner to avoid doing this as it can have some detrimental effects on your Business especially when you start expanding and employing staff members. As well as keeping a track of your regular cash flow, you must monitor your future financial forecast.

Just like using a map, a financial forecast guides you as you are taking your steps as a new Business. It helps you in achieving your Business goals and gives you a destination for your Business. The reality is that if you do not have a goal in mind when starting your Business, you will not be able to measure your rate of success. Another great importance of having a financial forecast for your new Business is that it helps you with effectively using the resources which are available to you. It gives you an overview of your whole company so you are able to prioritise your spending and use of resources at your disposal. It also helps you to control the spending in your company and this can in turn generate profit in your Business.

With your new Business, a financial projection is important especially if you are thinking of acquiring a loan or investment. The investor or Bank will need to know their return on investment and the future worth of the Business. Another benefit of having a financial forecast is that it can be changed and edited accordingly as time goes on. For example, if you prepare a financial forecast for the next one year, you can continually edit it as the year goes on and measure the forecast predicted against the actual results. This will help you to know whether you are performing well against your predicted numbers or you are falling below the targeted results.

Some of the advantages of keeping track of your numbers and having a financial forecast for your company are:

• As a new Business, you will need to know the viability of your Business. It will assist you in assessing the risk involved in starting your new Business and plan towards any 'bumps' that you may face along the way.

• It helps you to effectively plan the other parts of your Business model such as your marketing, advertising, promotion etc. Having a set budget in place in your financial statements will help to know what you can and cannot afford.

• Helps you to measure the performance of your company by measuring your actual performance against the projected target.

• It gives your Business a goal to work towards and it helps in keeping control of how money is spent in your Business so you don't end up in a loss.

• It will help you to know future cash injections that may be needed or any additional borrowings that may be needed so you can prepare for them and also prioritise the spending of the company.

• It also assists you in securing loans and investments for your Business. This is probably the most important piece of information which will be requested by your investor or lender.

• It gives you an idea of the break-even point in your Business especially when you are just starting off and investing your money into your Business, you would want to know which point you are able to start making a return on your investment.

One of the factors to consider when looking at your forecasts is how regular you need to prepare your financial statements. Usually as a new Business, you will develop an annual financial forecast for your Business; this will show you the viability of your idea and the health of your Business finances in the near future. As well as your yearly forecasts, monthly or weekly forecasts will also be highly beneficial as it helps you to set short term goals especially when you are just starting off. Having short term forecasts allows you to closely monitor your figures and develop strategies to counter any problems which may occur.

When putting together your financial statements, make sure the figures which you put down are realistic and achievable based on your capability and resources. Some of the figures can be determined using industry average figures. For example, when putting down your sales forecast for the future, you may not know how to predict this as a new Business, therefore you may need to look at your industry average to use in predicting yours.

Once you start running your Business and managing your finances, you will come across several words which you may not be familiar with. These words will be explained in much detail in this chapter. Let's start by looking at the terms 'Revenue' and 'Expenditure'.

Revenue

Revenue is sometimes referred to as 'Sales', 'Income' or 'Turnover'. This refers to the money which is generated by your company. In the simplest form, your revenue is the money which you make from selling your products or services to your customers.

You may come across two forms of revenue in your projections; the first one is the 'gross income'. Your gross income encapsulates all the money which your company takes in before any deductions are made. Deductions include the cost of running your Business, staff payment, interests and any other outgoing payments. These costs have already been examined in the last chapter. The second is the 'net income'. This refers to the money which is left over after you have made all the deductions from your gross income.

In order to calculate your projected turnover or revenue, you will look at all the sources of finance which you have chosen to use to start your Business and calculate the amount of products or services which you can sell within a certain period (e.g. one year). These will give you the total turnover for your company for that particular year. Always bear in mind that your revenue must be able to cover your total cost for that same period in your Business or else you will end up in a loss.

Expenditure

The last chapter examined the costs that will be incurred to you as a new Business owner and the importance of knowing the total cost of starting your company. These costs are known as expenditure, they are the expenses which your company will incur over a period of time.

Your projected expenditure will show all the costs that will be incurred towards your Business in the duration of the statement produced and this will help you to understand how much you will need in revenue to start up your Business. Similar to the revenue, there are two main types of expenditures that can appear in your cash flow statement, these are:

Capital Expenditure: These are the amounts that will be spent on acquiring long term assets. Your long term assets refers to those assets such as your building, land or any other equipment which will last over a long period and would be used for bringing in revenue into the company.
Each Business has its own set of capital expenditures and they would usually be those items which you will not use up during the period stated on your financial statement. For example, if you purchase computer equipment which will last you for the next two years and your cash flow statement only covers the next one year, then this will fall under the capital expenditure.

Revenue Expenditure: These are the costs which are incurred in the same period which your projections cover and they are also used up in the same period. These are the expenses that are used for day to day running of the Business. Such are salaries, wages, office supplies etc. These costs will appear on your regular profit and loss account against the money which you bring in during the same period.

These are the two main types of expenditures which will be found on your cashflow projections. It is very important to know the difference between these two.

The diagram in fig. 1.1 shows an example of the expenditure section of a cash flow statement. You can see that the diagram contains the two types of expenditures which are the revenue expenditure and the capital expenditure. The capital expenditure is listed below the revenue expenditure to separate the two types. You can list as many categories as you want for each one in your own cashflow projections. Again, this projection covers the period of one year as you can see and they are broken down into monthly figures.

BUDGET - YEAR 2		Month - 1	Month - 2	Month - 3	Month - 4	Month 5	Month - 6	Half Yr Tot	Month - 7	Month - 8	Month - 9	Month - 10	Month - 11	Month - 12	2nd Year Total
EXPENDITURE - REVENUE COSTS															
Bank Charges															
Standing Charges	1							0.00							0.00
Interest Payment	2							0.00							0.00
Other Charges	3							0.00							0.00
Total Bank Charges	**B**	0.00	0.00	0.00	0.00	0.00	0.00	0.00	0.00	0.00	0.00	0.00	0.00	0.00	0.00
Loan Repayments															
Standing Charges	1							0.00							0.00
Interest Payment	2							0.00							0.00
Other Charges	3							0.00							0.00
Total Loan Repayments	**C**	0.00	0.00	0.00	0.00	0.00	0.00	0.00	0.00	0.00	0.00	0.00	0.00	0.00	0.00
Staff Costs															
Staff Wages	1							0.00							0.00
Holiday Cover	2							0.00							0.00
Employers NIC	3							0.00							0.00
Volunteer Costs	4							0.00							0.00
Training Costs	5							0.00							0.00
Other Staff Costs	6							0.00							0.00
Total Staff Costs	**D**	0.00	0.00	0.00	0.00	0.00	0.00	0.00	0.00	0.00	0.00	0.00	0.00	0.00	0.00
Other Revenue Costs	**S**							0.00							0.00
TOTAL REVENUE COSTS	**T**	0.00	0.00	0.00	0.00	0.00	0.00	0.00	0.00	0.00	0.00	0.00	0.00	0.00	0.00
CAPITAL COSTS															
Refurbishment Costs	1							0.00							0.00
Major Office Equipment	2							0.00							0.00
Other Machinery Costs	3							0.00							0.00
Other Capital Costs	4							0.00							0.00
Asset Depreciation	5							0.00							0.00
TOTAL CAPITAL COSTS	**U**	0.00	0.00	0.00	0.00	0.00	0.00	0.00	0.00	0.00	0.00	0.00	0.00	0.00	0.00
					T = Q+ R+V										
TOTAL	**V**	0.00	0.00	0.00	0.00	0.00	0.00	0.00	0.00	0.00	0.00	0.00	0.00	0.00	0.00

Fig. 1.1

When projecting the numbers for your new Business, there are four main types of financial statements that you will use. They will come into play while planning your Business and when the Business is actually up and running, these are:

- Sales forecast

- Cashflow statement

- Profit and Loss account

- Balance sheet

ACTION POINTS

After gaining a better understanding of the differences between Revenue and Expenditure, the next step is to understand these two terms in relation to your own idea.

1. List down all the different revenue streams for your new Business.

2. List down the different expenditures which you will come across in your new Business. Break them down into the Capital and Revenue Expenditure.

Sales Forecast

Your sales forecast is where you get the opportunity to put down your projections for the sales of your goods or services. This will allow you to set targets for the amount of money which you want to generate from the sales of your products or services over a period of time.

Your sales forecast will help you with creating your cashflow statement. With the sales forecast, you have to list down the month by month or weekly sales target which you aim to meet once your Business is up and running. This can be written down by categorising your products or services or you can write it down for each product or service which you provide.

It goes without saying that your sales forecast must be realistic and achievable. It must reflect the other strategies which you have stated for your company such as your marketing strategies. There's no point in forecasting figures which you know you cannot realistically meet as this will defeat the whole purpose of creating one in the first place.

As a new Business, you will be creating your sales forecast based on assumptions but they must be based on research which you have carried out such as market trends, average sales within your market or industry etc. When you are creating your sales forecast, you can either categorise your products or services by the type of customer which you aim to sell to or by the product or service.

For example, if you are a web designer, you could list your sales forecast against the different packages which you provide or the different customers which you aim to sell to. Below is an example of what it can look like:

Forecasting by service category:

Item Name	January
Website package 1	£2000
Website Package 2	£2500
Website Package 3	£1500

With this type of forecast, you have decided to use your service category against the sales forecast. You have listed the category of websites which you provide and listed the sales predictions or targets next to them. The example above shows that you aim to make a total of £6000 in the month of January and you have broken these down into the different packages and how much you aim to sell from each package in that month. This only shows the month of January but you will have to do the same for the rest of the year and this will show your final sales forecast both in each category and for the total website packages.

Customer Category	January
Councils	£ 5000
StartUp Businesses	£1500
Small Businesses	£2000

With the example shown above, it is similar to the first method of forecasting in sales figures. The only difference is that this example uses the category of your customers as the method for listing down the sales forecasts. With this example, you have to know the different types of customers which you will be dealing with as a new Business and you can place a sales prediction or target next to each one to show how much you want to make from each one within that time period.

As well as writing down the predicted figures for each month in your sales forecast, another figure which you may want to include is the units or volume which you intend to sell in that month. By doing this, you are able to know how much resources or costs are involved in production to achieve the sales figure predicted. This will also enable you to know the required sales in that month in order to reach the target. An example of this is stated below:

Item Name	Units Sold	Price	January
Website package 1	5	£400	£2000
Website Package 2	2	£1250	£2500
Website Package 3	1	£1500	£1500

The example above doesn't only show the sales figures this time but it also shows how many website packages need to be sold in that particular month in order to achieve the set target. You can use the same format for your own Business where you list down the volume or units which you aim to sell every month. You may decide to break down your sales forecast by product or service type, packages, customers or by location.

The point of creating the sales forecast is to form part of your whole financial statement which will be reviewed as your Business progresses and the actual figures compared against it to measure the progress of the company.
There are several types of sales forecasting software which can be bought or ones which you can create yourself on Database systems.

Cashflow Statement

A cashflow statement holds information about your revenue and expenditure. The main point of creating a cashflow statement is that it shows all the money coming in and going out of your Business. Your sales forecast can also form part of your cashflow statement.

The format of the cashflow statement is very similar to the sales forecast. The only difference is that a cashflow statement doesn't only show incoming money but it also shows you the outgoing money. The point of this is so that you can measure your spending against your income to know the health of your Business within the period of your cashflow statement.

Just like the sales forecast, a cashflow statement will state the month by month or week by week financial health of your company. This depends on your choice of breakdown. It is impossible to know how much money you have to spend or how much money will be available at any point in your Business if you do not have the cash flow statement which helps with understanding the revenue that is coming in regularly and how it is being spent.

As a new Business, your cash flow will allow you to know what to prioritise when spending and will help you to effectively manage your finances. Whether your

Business is a one man Business or you will be hiring employees, it is imperative that you develop your cash flow system for the next year or so in your Business as this will give everyone involved in your Business a guide to follow and help to measure performances.

When creating a cashflow statement you don't necessarily need a fancy software or a special accounting knowledge to do it, there are several templates available online which can be downloaded to suit your company's needs or you can use programs such as spreadsheets. You must make sure that you revise your cashflow statement when your Business is up and running so you can measure the performance of the Business against projected performances at the start.

This will help you to know areas to work on and hence give you a sense of direction. When putting together your cash flow statement, there are three questions you need to ask yourself:

⇨   What revenue figures am I expecting in that period? You need to be realistic with yourself and state down the total amount of money which would be coming into your Business in the period which you are preparing the statement for.

   Your projections must reflect your marketing capacities. For example, there is no point of you projecting that you will be making £100000 a month as a web designer if you are the only employee of the company because you do not have the capacity to take on such amount of work and probably haven't got the marketing resources to pull in such amount of money in your first year. Your income figures must be realistic.

⇨   What is my revenue expenditure? As already mentioned, this refers to the cost incurred in the daily running of your Business. You must look at all the costs which are likely to be incurred even if it is a low amount as it all adds up at the end of the year.

⇨   What is my capital expenditure? This has also been discussed earlier. You must know what your capital expenditure is. What are those costs which would last longer than the period of the cash flow statement?

These are the questions which you should be thinking about when putting your cash flow statement together as they will guide you with accumulating your figures.

ACTION POINTS

The diagram in fig. 1.2 shows an example of a cashflow statement for the next 6 months. This will give you an idea of what your cashflow may look like. You can see that the top half of the table includes the revenue, stating the different products and the amount which they will be bringing in during the 6 month period. The lower half also contains the expenditure which shows the spending during this same period.

Your cashflow doesn't have to look exactly like this and your categories may vary, but this gives you an idea of what your cashflow may look like.

The 'Cash Flow' section at the bottom of the template represents the subtraction of your expenditure from your revenue for each month.
Your 'Cash Balance' refers to the total amount of money that is brought forward from the previous month, added together with the Cash Flow amount for that month.

1. Using the example of the template given below, create your own cashflow statement for the next year of your Business. (Remember that a cashflow statement can be created for one year, two years or five years. It depends on the period you want to cover)

2. Use the expenditures and revenues you have stated in previous action points to fill out the revenues and expenditures in your cash flow.

First 6 Month Cash Flow For year starting (mm yy):							
	Month						First Half Total
Revenue							
Product 1							
Product 2							
Product 3							
Product 4							
Product 5							
Product 6							
Product 7							
Product 8							
Product 9							
Product 10							
Total Revenue							
Expenditure							
Production Cost							
Cost of Sales							
Professional and Legal Fees							
Technology and Equipment Costs							
Administrative Costs							
Building and Premises Costs							
Marketing Costs							
Staff / Employee							
Extra Category:							
Extra Category:							
Extra Category:							
Total Expenditure							
Cash Flow	-	-	-	-	-	-	-
Cash Balance	-	-	-	-	-	-	-

Fig 1.2

The Balance Sheet

As a Business start up, a Balance sheet is another financial statement that you need to get accustomed to. This financial statement can be used at any point in your Business, both at the start-up and when the Business is up and running.

It gives you 'a snapshot' of the financial health of your Business at any given point in your Business. You can either do a forecast Balance sheet or prepare one at the end of an accounting period. Your balance sheet will show you the financial state of your Business within the period stated on it. So for example, your Balance sheet could contain the state of your finances over the last one year of trading if you have been trading for a year or it can contain the forecast which you predict in the first one year of your Business. When it comes to creating a starting Balance Sheet, your figures must be accurate as this will help you to analyse the financial outlook of your new Business.

The contents of your Balance sheet will be different from that of the Cashflow forecast. Your balance sheet is made up of three sections:

- Assets: These are items owned by the company which have monetary value.

- Liabilities: These are debts which are owed by the company during the process of acquiring the assets.

- Equity: This is the amount which you have invested into the Business either at the start or during the course of the Business venture.

The Balance sheet gives you an idea of how the money invested in the Business will be spent. It tells you the assets which your finances will be spent on. The resources which you will be acquiring to start up your New Business will fall under the 'assets' categories and the finance methods which you have chosen to use for your new Business will either fall under liabilities or equities.

This depends whether the money will be coming from your personal cash injection or money borrowed from other sources. This is where you need to know how the money borrowed will be spent. The balance sheet also helps you to know if your personal finance is enough to start a successful Business or you need to borrow some more money from creditors.Depending on the type of company you have decided to form (e.g. sole trader or Private Company), your Balance sheet may be one of the documents needed for filing your annual accounts.Therefore it will be good to get used to the process of creating one right from the start of your new Business.

Your balance sheet would tell you whether you need to put more money into your Business or the money being invested in are enough to start the new venture. When you are starting off, you must know all the items and resources needed and we have already dealt with this in previous chapters. This can be judged against the total money which the company has coming in.

Below is a formula that you need to be familiar with when dealing with the issue of creating your balance sheet:

$$Assets - Liabilities = Equity$$

This equation simply shows you that the money which your company owes, subtracted from the total cash and items owned by your company equals your total equity.

Let us examine some of the terminologies that you will find in a Balance sheet. As a Business owner, whether you choose to take care of your day to day company accounts or you choose to hand the responsibility over to an Accountant, you must still be familiar with these terminologies:

Assets

As previously mentioned, your assets are those items which belong to the company or those which you need in order to start your Business and they have a monetary value. Assets are divided into Current and Long Term (or fixed assets).

A. **Current assets:** They are short term assets whose values can fluctuate on a day to day basis. With these types of assets, they can be converted to cash within the same year. They are the assets which are expected to be used, sold or consumed within a year. Your current assets fund the day to day operations of your Business and also pay for the expenses which occur in the day to day running of your Business. These current assets can range from cash toforeign currency and it all depends on the nature of your Business. Here are some common examples of current assets:

• Cash

In a Balance sheet, 'cash' refers to the amount of money which you expect to have in your bank account at the beginning of your Business. This could include savings, payroll accounts and other types of accounts which your company may own as well as any other petty cash which you may have on hand. This is the money which is available immediately for use once the Business starts running.

• Debtors

As a new Business, this may apply to you if your sales are made on credit terms (i.e. your customers are able to pay for your goods or services by obtaining credit from you and paying over a period of time). The 'debtors' section of the balance sheet refers to the money which customers, suppliers and other vendors owe your company. As a new Business with no previous transactions with customers or suppliers, you will not have any entries here in your starting Balance Sheet.

• Stock / Inventory:
Your Stock, otherwise referred to as inventory, are the goods which your company owns and are ready to be distributed or sold. They are those items waiting to be sold to customers. For the owner of a convenience store, his stock is the sweets and chocolates that are left on the shelves which have not been sold yet and those in the backroom.

For the builder, his stock will be the pieces of wood which are yet to be used up but are kept in storage. As a new Business, you will have stock which you are going to purchase or make and this is where you state those stocks. Your type of stock will depend on the type of Business you have.

• Prepayment:
Prepayments are those payments which you make for goods and services which you may not receive before the end of the accounting year. These are payments which you make in advance, hoping to get the service or products at a later day.

Examples of this are insurance premiums which are paid in advance for the whole year. For example, if you were to take out an insurance policy and paid a premium of £1200 for the whole year, this would count as a prepayment in your Balance sheet. As each month goes past, you will account for the £100 which covers that month as expenses in your profit and loss account.

Your prepayments can also be membership subscriptions etc. As a new Business, your prepayments will be the expenses which you have to pay before the opening of your Business; these could even include paying in advance for some utilities etc. As long as the service or product you are paying for has not been supplied yet, it counts as a prepayment.

• **Notes receivables:** These are quite unusual. They are written promises to receive particular sums of money on a future date. An example of notes receivable is where you offer your products or services to a customer and they promise in writing to pay off the money over a period of time. In order for this to count as a current asset, the payment period agreed must fall within the period stated on the balance sheet.If it doesn't, then it counts as a fixed or long term asset. As a Business Start-Up, it is not likely that you will have any note receivables as you have not started trading. This can only apply if you have been taken on some freelance work before you started your new Business.

• **Other Current Assets:** These are other current assets which have not been listed above which may apply to your Business:

Total Current/Short Term Assets: This is where you state the total amount of your short term or current assets which you have stated for your new Business.

B. **LongTerm / Fixed assets:** These are the properties which belong to your company and are used in the production of your goods or services but are not expected to be used up in the period which is included in your Balance sheet. These include land, buildings, machinery, and vehicles which are used in connection with the business. Fixed assets are broken down further into two types. These are Tangible and intangible fixed assets.

As the name denotes, tangible assets are those fixed assets which can be touched and felt such as buildings, land etc. Intangible assets are those which cannot be felt or touched but still come under the category of fixed assets. These can include Goodwill, patents, trademark, domain registration, etc., which lasts over the period stated in the Balance sheet.

• **Tangible Fixed Assets:**

Land
If you decide to purchase a piece of land for your new Business, the amount for this will be entered here. If you are taking over an existing land from a previous owner, then you will need to find out what the value of the land is and enter it here. The land which you intend on purchasing will count as a fixed asset.

Buildings
Your building or premises will only come under the fixed assets category if it is owned by you. If you are renting or leasing it, then it wouldn't apply to this

category.

Office equipment
Make a list of office equipments that you are going to buy which will last longer than the period stated on your Balance sheet. E.g., PhotoCopiers, fax machines, printers and computers which will be used for your Business.

Machinery
This entry will apply to Businesses which make use of plants for manufacturing or producing their products. The machinery which you intend to use will be stated here and the value for this will be stated in this section. An example of this is a printing press.

Vehicles
If you are using a company vehicle for your Business, then the price of acquiring that vehicle will go into this section.

Other Tangible fixed Asset
These are the tangible fixed assets which have not been listed above but may apply to your Business.

• Intangible Fixed Assets:

Goodwill: Goodwill usually applies to you if you are taking over the Business from someone else or upon incorporation of an existing sole trader Business. These are the intangible assets such as telephone number, Business name, Website domain name and other items that have been passed on to you by the previous owner of the Business. These will usually add value to your business and is passed on by the previous owner.

Patents: This is a form of intellectual property. It protects the process and method which you use in producing your products and services. Any patent which you have taken will be listed under this category.

Trademark: This is a symbol or sign which signifies that a product or service or name has been officially and legally restricted to the use of the owner or manufacturer.

Other Intangible Fixed Assets: These are the other intangible fixed assets which have not been listed in the categories above.

• **Total Fixed or Long Term Assets:** This contains all the total amount of your long term or fixed assets, adding together all the tangible and intangible assets.

C. **Total Assets:** This is the addition of all your assets. These will include your current and long term assets.

ACTION POINTS

1. Make a list of all the Current Assets in your new Business.

2. Make a list of all the Fixed or Long Term Assets in your Business.

3. Write down the amount of each item next to it.

4. Calculate your total assets.

Liabilities

Liabilities are money owed to creditors for transactions which have taken place. As a start-up, it is obvious that you will need to acquire some resources for your new Business as previously stated. Acquiring these resources may mean that you borrow some money from others. These money owed will fall under the 'liabilities' section of your balance sheet.

Your liabilities include debts and money which are owed to outside creditors such as banks, loans, mortgages and other ways which you have chosen to finance your Business that will incur a debt. In previous chapters, we looked at several ways of financing your Business and you should have chosen the right method for acquiring your assets. If you have gone through the 'Bootstrapping' path, then you may not have any liability, otherwise you need to look at the liabilities in your new Business right from the start.

Similar to your assets, the liabilities are also divided into long term and short term liabilities. Here are some liabilities that you may come across:

A. **Current Liabilities:** Your current liabilities are those debts and obligations which your company needs to pay within the time frame of the period stated. These are also known as short term liabilities. As a new Business, you must be aware of all the short term liabilities which you will incur during the first year of your Business so that you can put plans in place to cover them.

• **Creditors:** The Creditors section of your balance sheet will contain those payments owed to creditors, suppliers etc, which needs to be paid during the period of your Balance sheet. These are money owed where a service has been provided for you on credit. As a new Business, you may have some creditors at the start of your Business such as advertising costs, costs of acquiring stock, etc.

If these items have not been paid for, and it is due within the first year of the Balance sheet, then it will fall under this section. If you are taking over a previously owned Business, then you may inherit some old accounts which may be transferred to you as the new owner.

• **Notes payable:** These are the money which you have promised to pay to lenders within the year stated in your Balance sheet. This could be money borrowed from family, friends etc. The point of notes payable is that it needs to be paid back within a short time and this is agreed in writing to know when the payments will be made.

• **Short Term loans and overdrafts:** One of the ways which you could have chosen to fund your Business is by applying for an overdraft or some other type of short term loans which will be paid back within the first financial year. These loans will be stated in this section. Remember that once the payments cross over the one year period, then it becomes a long tern liability.

• **Taxes:** Taxes are also part of your short term liabilities. These are obligations which your company would have to pay within the year. The taxes which you may have to pay are National Insurance, VAT and PAYE. VAT will only apply to you if you chose to be registered for it and PAYE will apply once you register yourself or another person as an employee of the company. Another kind of tax is the Corporation tax.

• **Wages:** This also applies to you if you plan to employ staff members. The best way to predict this is to look at how much you wish to pay the staff members and use this as the basis for predicting the wages.

• **Accruals:** These are sometimes referred to as accrued expenses. They refer to the goods and services which you have already used up but haven't yet been billed for. For example, your electricity bill comes in every three months and a certain bill covered 3 months ending on the 30th of April. If your Balance sheet covers the year up to 31st March, it means that you are going to have to account for the two months which you have used up in the period before the 31st April when the bill has not yet been sent to you. The best way to handle this is to 'accrue' a portion of your three months bill so it can appear on your Balance sheet that ended on the 31st of March and carry over the remaining month to the next year's balance sheet. An example of a way to do this is:

Electricity Bill Period: 1st February   –   30th April
Estimate Charge (Based on previous Bills)   -   £500 (Three months bill)
Period that falls within the Balance sheet   -   1st February – 31st March

Bill accrued for the Balance sheet period = $\dfrac{£500}{3\ \text{months}}$ *** 2 months = £333.3**

From the breakdown above, you can see that the accrued amount is £333.3 which means that the two months can be entered into the Balance sheet even though an invoice hasn't been produced yet. As a new Start-Up, you may not have an accrual until you actually start trading. If you do, then you will state them here.

• Other Current Liabilities: There are other short term liabilities which you may want to add to your Balance sheet but haven't been stated above.

• Total current liabilities: This refers to the total amount which you have predicted on your current liabilities. They are the total money to be paid out in the first year predicted in your Balance sheet.

B. Long-term liabilities: These are any debts or obligations owed by the business which are due more than one year from the start of your Business.

• **Long Term Notes / Creditors:** These are the loans or credits which are not going to be paid off within one year. These include Bank loans, Finance agreements etc. You need to list down all the credits which you owe and know you owe and know you cannot in the short term. Any money borrowed to be invested in the Business and repaid over a long period will go into this section.

• **Mortgage Payables:** This is the balance which is going to be left on your mortgage at the period stated on your Balance sheet. For example if your property is worth £500000 and your mortgage is £400000, then the £400000 goes into this section while the value of the property goes into your assets. As a Start-up, you need to state the amount you owe in mortgage in this section at the beginning of your Business.

• **Other Long-term liabilities:** This will contain any other long term liability that has not been mentioned in the categories above.

• **Total Long Term Liabilities:** This will contain the total amount of the amount which you owe creditors over a long period of time.

C. **Total Liabilities:** This will contain the total debt and obligations owed by the company at the start of trading. This will show you the total amount which you will have to pay out in the first year and beyond.

D. **Owner's equity:** Any money which you have put into financing your Business up to the point of actually running it will appear in this section. If you are buying an existing Business, then the amount you bought the Business for should appear in this section. This will basically contain your financial input into the company. All loans and any other investments should not go into this field

---

<u>ACTION POINTS</u>

1. List down all your liabilities in your new Business.
   • Make a list of all the Current Liabilities in your new Business.

   • Make a list of all the Long Term liabilities in your Business.

   • Write down the amount of each item next to it.

   • Calculate your total Liabilities.

2. State your 'Owners Equity' in your Business as described in the main text.

E. **Total Liability and Equity:** This is the total amount of money which has been used to finance your Business in order to start it off. This will show you how much you have put into the Business in total and how much you will be spending in the first year and subsequent years.

According to the law, your Balance sheet must contain your Current Assets, Fixed Assets, Current Liabilities and Long Term liabilities. The content in these categories can vary and depends on the type of Business you are going into but the four categories must be present. The main point of a Balance sheet is for both sides to be equal to one another. I.e. your total assets should be equal to your total liability and equity. If this does not occur, then, you may seek the help of a professional or look at some items that may be missing.

What you do not want from the start of your Business is to find yourself in the negative where the money you have spent is more than the value of items owned by your company. Doing your Balance sheet will help you assess this.

ACTION POINTS

The diagram in fig. 1.3 shows a simple Balance Sheet Template. There are several types of template that can be acquired but the contents will stay the same. All the contents under each category will be different as they will include your Business assets and liabilities.

1. Using the assets and liabilities which you have already stated in previous action tasks, create your own Balance Sheet for the next year, stating the assets, liabilities, equity.

2. Ensure that the Total Assets and the Total liability plus Equity are equal to one another. (If you have any problems creating this, you may seek professional assistance).

Balance Sheet for Year Ending (mm yy):			
Assets	**Amount**	**Liabilities**	**Amount**
Current Assets	-	**Current Liabilities**	
Cash		Accounts Payable	
Accounts Receivables		Notes Payable	
Stocks/Inventory		Short Term loans and Overdrafts	
Prepayments		Taxes	
Notes Receivables		Wages	
Other Current Assets		Accruals	
		Other Current Liabilities	
Total Current Assets		**Total Current Liabilities**	
Fixed Assets	-	**Long Term Liabilities**	
Tangible Fixed Assets		Long Term Notes/Creditors	
Land		Mortgage Payables	
Buildings		Other Long Term Liabilities	
Office Equipments			
Machinery			
Vehicles			
Other Tangible Fixed Assets			
Intangible Fixed Assets			
Goodwill			
Patents			
Trademark			
Long Term Investment			
Other Intangible Fixed Assets			
Total Fixed Assets		**Total Long Term Liabilities**	
		Total Liabilities	
		Owners Equity	
Total Assets		**Total Liabilities and Equity**	

Income statement

An income statement is also known as your Profit and Loss account. The main purpose of this financial statement is to project the expenditures and revenues which will be coming in and out of your Business over a period of time. This statement and your Balance sheet combined are the most important statements which you must have especially for applying for funding or investment. The period of time covered in your income statement tends to be one year.

At the beginning of your Business, it is advisable to create at least a one year income statement as this will assist you when seeking investment or loans. This will ensure that you are able to present the projected financial state of your Business to the potential investor. Your income statement will record all your income or revenue during the first year and will also look at your operating cost in the same year. The main point of this statement is to subtract your costs from your income in order to calculate your profit or losses.

Creating a projected income statement helps to predict the revenues and expenses of your Business over a particular time. As a Business owner, you may want to know where you are overspending and where you are spending below the budget. This statement will allow you to do so. It is very important as it can allow you to set budgets for your coming year and allows you to then weigh it against the actual spending so that you can know your variance over a period of time. Your variance refers to the difference between your budget and your actual spending in the given period on your profit and loss account.

With your income statement, if used regularly, you will be able to pinpoint the little amounts which can cause big problems in the overall financial outlook of your company. These types of amounts include costs such as phone line rental etc. They are the costs they may not look like a lot but accumulate over time if they are not monitored. Therefore your income statement will allow you to monitor them over the period of time.

Similarly with the Balance Sheet and Cashflow statement, there are various templates available which can assist you in creating your profit and loss account. It is up to you to make sure that you find one which is easy to use and easy to understand for you and your company. There are several words which tend to come up in income statements. Here are some of them:

1. **Sales:** The sales section of an income statement will represent every income that will be generated by your Business during the trading year. You have already

predicted this in your sales forecast, so this section will be made easier once your sales forecast is already in place.

2. **Cost of Goods sold/ Production cost:** As previously stated, this refers to the costs which are directly involved in producing your products and services. This includes the purchase of raw materials from suppliers which will be used in producing the goods or the internal expenses that may be included in delivering your service to your customers.

3. **Gross Profit / Margin:** This is calculated by subtracting your total sales from the production costs. This does not include any taxes or operating expenses which will be coming up next. Your gross profit is simply looking at the margin which you will derive at after subtracting your sales forecast from your cost of making the products. It is important to make sure that this figure is high as it means you are making enough money from your product or service after you have paid for the production and there is still enough money to cover other expenses and overhead.

After covering all the expenses, the Business still needs to have enough money left over. If you find that this number is low, then you are either charging too low for your products or services or you are paying too much for your production costs.

4. **Operating Expenses:** This is otherwise known as your revenue expenditure. We have already discussed this earlier. It refers to the costs incurred from the daily running of your Business. Here are some examples of operating expenses:

a. **Salaries:** The salaries and bonuses which you pay yourself and your staff members.

b. **Marketing / Sales/ Promotional Materials:** These are the cost incurred in the purchasing and creating of your sales and marketing materials. These could include free giveaways, fliers and any other materials that are needed for promoting your company.

c. **Advertising:** These include all the cost involved with advertising of your company.

d. **Travel:** These are the costs which you or your staff members incur when travelling on Business duties. This is particularly important for Businesses that involve visiting customers outside of the office premises.

e. **Rent:** The monthly or regular rent paid towards your premises.

f. **Utilities:** Your utilities include water, gas, electricity, Business rates and all other utilities associated with running your Business.

g. **Depreciation:** These are the expenses which have to be considered when looking at the value of the equipments used in your Business. These equipments could be losing value over time and therefore the depreciated part will be written here.

h. **Overhead costs:** Your overhead costs are those items that you may not be able to place under any category listed above but still fall under expenses. These include insurance, office supplies etc.

5. **Capital Expenses:** Some Businesses choose to separate the capital and operating expenses. Examples of these include, Office Building, Refurbishment, Major office Equipments etc. It's up to you to separate this or put them under the same category.

6. **Income before Tax:** This refers to the total expenses subtracted from the gross profit. This is the income which will belong to your company after deducting the expenses and production costs before tax is charged. Note that this figure can be deceptively optimistic as it makes your profit looks way bigger than it is. Therefore it is important to consider your reductions such as taxes.

7. **Taxes:** This is the amount which is due to be paid to the Government from your Business.

8. **Net Profit:** This is also referred to as your Net income, Net Earnings, Current Earnings etc. This number is derived after you have subtracted the total taxes to be paid from the 'income before tax'. This is the total profit which belongs to your company after taxes have been paid. This number can either be positive or negative and if you find that it is negative, then your company will be making a loss in the first year and this is where you have to look at all the costs and find out where some cuts can be made to the costs or some increase can be made to the sales.

These are just some of the types of words which can come up in your profit and loss account and the explanations given above will help you in gaining an understanding of these words once you come across them in your Business.

As mentioned earlier, there are several ways in which an Income Statement can be used in your Business, you can either use it as a day to day tool in your Business or you can also use it for projecting the first few years of your Business and know the financial prospect of your company if it is likely to make a profit or loss in the first few years.

When creating your profit and loss account, it is important to set sales target or cost budgets and also note the actual figures achieved during the time specified in the statement and this will help you to know the variance during that period. This will help you to know where you are exceeding the targets set.

As a new Business, it is advisable to do this monthly so you can constantly check the financial wellbeing of your company regularly and deal with any issues which may cause a problem in the future.

An example of such profit and loss account has been given in Fig 1.4 which shows you how to set targets and budgets and check for actual results. The space for 'comments' given in the last column gives you the opportunities to write down any issues that may have caused the negative or positive variance for each category in the period stated. For example, we overspent on the utilities cost budget because our gas bill was increased since last month. This will help you to tackle every issue that may come up and allow your whole company to understand the state of the finances in the company as a whole.

ONE YEAR PROJECTED INCOME STATEMENT				
Year Ending mm yy:				
	Budget	Actual	Variance	Comments
INCOME (Excluding Capital)				
Sales	0.00			
Item 1	0.00			
Item 2	0.00			
Item 3	0.00			
Item 4	0.00			
Total INCOME (Excluding Capital)	0.00			
PRODUCTION COSTS				
Shipping				
Raw Materials				
Total PRODUCTION COSTS	0.00			
Gross Income	0.00			
COSTS				
Revenue Costs				
Bank Charges	0.00			
Loan Repayments	0.00			
Staff Costs	0.00			
Travel Costs	0.00			
Premises Costs	0.00			
Utilities Costs	0.00			
Insurance Costs	0.00			
Computer Hardware	0.00			
Office Furniture	0.00			
Administration Costs	0.00			
Food & Drinks	0.00			
Marketing / Advertising	0.00			
Professional Fees	0.00			
Total Revenue Costs	0.00			
Capital Costs				
Refurbishment Costs	0.00			
Major Office Equipment	0.00			
Other Capital Costs	0.00			
Asset Depreciation	0.00			
Total Capital Costs	0.00			
Total COSTS	0.00			
Income Before Tax	0.00			
Tax	0.00			
NET INCOME	0.00			

Fig 1.4

ACTION POINTS

You have learnt the different aspects of the income statement and you have seen an example in Fig 1.4.

1. Using the example given in Fig 1.4 as a guideline, create an Income statement for the first year of trading in your Business.

2. Project whether you will make a profit or loss.

After looking at the three main statements that you will come across when projecting the numbers in your new Business, you should have become more familiar with these and using them shouldn't be an issue for you throughout your Business journey.

If you find yourself struggling with creating any of these statements, get some professional help as these statements are important in the planning and projection of your new Business. This applies especially if you aim to seek funding or investment.

GET UP AND DO SOMETHING

I had to make my own living and my own opportunity! But I made it! Don't sit down and wait for the opportunities to come. Get up and make them!

.J. WALKER

Once you have gone through the steps which have been laid out in this book and you have applied all the concepts discussed in each chapter to your idea. You may still wonder the next steps to take in turning your ideas into a reality.

Well, here are some practical steps which you can take once you have developed the plan for your idea.

Get Some Help!

There is no one in this world who knows it all. If you find that you are stuck on the next step to take with regards to your idea, seek help. Get a coach, mentor, advisor etc. Ask people around you for help. When I mean get some help, I don't mean attend seminars, take note and do nothing about it. I am talking about practical hands on help. Get someone who can work with you side by side on the idea and helps you on your way to realising the idea. This is one of the great advantages of having a coach. A coach motivates you, pushes you, guides you, encourages and supports you through your entrepreneurial journey.

Every top sportsperson has a coach, why shouldn't a top Business person get one as well? If you need help moving forward, seek the right help to ensure you get to your destination.

Network!, Network!!, Network!!!

I cannot stress the importance of networking enough. Especially for a start-up, networking is crucial to the progress of your Business and for your self-development. Starting a new Business or project can be a lonely journey and this is why you must ensure that you surround yourself with other people who are on the same journey, who can also encourage you through the start-up journey.

This is one of the reasons why I created the Business Start-Up academy to give start-ups a platform to regularly network and meet other start-ups who can work with them through their journey.

Networking is all about building relationships, meeting people who can impact your Business, meeting potential investors and building contacts who can be useful to your Business either now or in the future.

Set a Launch Date

One of the steps discussed in this book is all about goal setting. Setting a launch date for your New Business means that you are working towards a defined goal.

This means that you can plan towards that goal which you have set and you can set out all the tasks to be completed before the set date.

I have met many people who have set out Business plans for a long time but end up doing nothing about them. Failure to set a launch date means that you may take longer than you should to get your Business off the ground. One of the first steps that I take with new clients is to set a launch date for their new Business before taking any step.

Take Action

This is the most important step that you can take which will help you realise your passion or ideas. Get out there and start selling your products or services.

Make mistakes, hit bumps throughout your journey but whatever you do, make sure that you keep moving and heading in the right direction.

ACTION POINTS

After reading the practical steps that you can take to turn your passion into your Profession and going through the steps highlighted in this book,

1. What practical steps are you going to take now to get your ideas off the ground?

2. Make a list of these steps.

<u>AFTERWORD</u>

'Turn Your passion Into Your Profession' is a much needed book in these times. The last decade has truly shaken the world Economic systems and a lot of people who thought they had jobs for life no longer feel safe. Even those who have secured jobs at the moment are looking for ways to subsidise their wages. This is where this book comes to play for those looking 'to do their own thing', so to speak

This is a well thought out and well written book which gives a comprehensive guide to both new and existing business owners as to how to, not only set up but also to manage their businesses.

Passion is something that a lot of people take for granted but it is one of those things which is there to help our purpose. The author has taken time to digest ways in which to acknowledge what we are good at and how to let it work for us.

Having a profession is certainly one of the surest ways forward in this current economic climate. Working for oneself is obviously not for everyone but for those who choose to go through this route, this book is probably the best step by step guide for business owners I have read in recent times. This is because it has been written almost as a foolproof guide and is evidently very easy to understand. It is also clearly up to date with regards to technological changes that one must be aware of when embarking on a business journey in this modern world.

Because the author has been running the 'Business start up Academy', he has come across a lot of issues which cripple people in their entrepreneurial journey and has set out to find solutions for such problems. All the questions I had were answered as I read through the chapters.

There are people who may have experiences in some areas of running a business but lack knowledge in other areas such as book keeping. This book has managed to cover every possible area that may be encountered in the business world so that nothing is overlooked.

As an individual with an accounting background, I was most impressed with the way the author had simplified the accounting side of this book so that even if you do not intend to hire an accountant, you could practically manage your books yourself.

Having read this book cover to cover, I personally feel motivated and charged to Turn my passion into something even greater.

It has been easy to read and a joy to learn at the same time as I am sure prospective readers will also find.

J. Opoku

Editor, El Shaddai Publishers

About The Author

Opy Onas is simply known as "The Midwife". He has a unique ability to unlock the hidden potentials within any individual and bring their ideas to life. He is an Entrepreneur, Business Start-Up Coach, keynote speaker, writer and author.

He is a skilled and enthusiastic trainer, running seminars and workshops, and delivering coaching programmes to businesses and youth organisations. Opy has the ability to connect with audiences from diverse backgrounds and age groups ranging between 7 – 50 years old. Everyone that comes across Opy immediately senses his passion and ability to deliver in a unique fashion.

He is the founder of Proten International, a Business Start-Up coaching company which helps individuals across the world develop and set up new Businesses. He is also the founder of the Business start-up academy where individuals develop their ideas and build new Business with other aspiring entrepreneurs.

He has a strong belief that every individual is impregnated with an idea and it only takes the right person to unlock the idea and bring it to life. Having started his first

Business at the age of 22, Opy decided to use his experience and knowledge gained to help individuals internationally find their passion and turn it into a successful business.

To book Opy for Speaking Engagements or enquire about any of his services, please email:

hello@opyonas.com or call (+44) 207 183 7328.

Visit his website at www.opyonas.com

Join the Proten One-One Coaching Programme

⇨ Do you have a Business Idea and you're not sure what to do next?
⇨ Are you a new Business owner who wants to take your Business to the next level?

Join the Proten One-One Business Start-Up coaching Programme today! The experienced and professional coaches at Proten are ready to help you take your idea to the next level.

- Turn your Business idea into a reality.

- Receive support, guidance, encouragement and motivation through your start-up process.

- Reach your goals faster than you would on your own.

- Choose from our range of established coaches.

Visit www.protenuk.com today to find out how you can join this Programme.

Email info@protenuk for more information.

Join the Business Start-Up Academy

- Develop your Business ideas

- Build your Business with other aspiring entrepreneurs

- Showcase your products / services to other entrepreneurs

- Develop your confidence and enhance your Business skills

- Network with other aspiring entrepreneurs

- Learn from existing Business owners and experts.

Join the Business Start-Up Academy today!

The Business Start-Up Academy can also be delivered at schools, colleges, universities, churches, prisons and youth organisations.

Visit **www.start-upacademy.co** to find out more or email **info@start-upacademy. co**

Lightning Source UK Ltd.
Milton Keynes UK
UKOW042129291212

204204UK00002B/19/P